A BANQUET OF
HEALTH

D0089867

BY
PENNY BLOCK

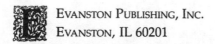
EVANSTON PUBLISHING, INC.
EVANSTON, IL 60201

EVANSTON PUBLISHING, INC.
1571 SHERMAN AVENUE, ANNEX C
EVANSTON, IL 60201

Evanston Publishing, Inc. certifies that the recipes in this book to are not intended as a medically therapeutic program, nor as a substitute for medically approved diet plans for people on fat-, cholesterol-, sugar-, or sodium-restricted diets. You should consult your physician before beginning any diet plan.

Printed in the U.S.A.

10 9 8 7 6 5 4 3 2

ISBN: 1-879260-28-X

Table of Contents

Foreword.. 5

Preface: Guidelines for Food Selection........................ 8

Introduction 12

Glossary of Ingredients and Food Items 47

Buying Sources 50

Appetizers 53

Soups.. 59

Grains & Pasta 81

Legumes... 111

Tofu & Tempeh.. 121

Seitan & Fu 128

Vegetables 134

Salads 144

Sauces, Dips & Dressings 149

Sea Vegetables 159

Fish... 167

Sweets 176

Seasonal Menu Suggestions 201

Appendix 206

Index 211

To my husband, Keith, for his inspiration and unflagging encouragement, and to my children, Carla, Shana, Ben, and Julie, for their immense patience with my kitchen experimentation.

FOREWORD

Eating well means you are choosing to create a healthful, dynamic life-style.

Eating well does not mean you are giving up the excitement of the eating experience.

As you will see, Penny Block's *Banquet of Health* is a book that illuminates, guides, and challenges you toward a healthy, dynamic life-style that provides the body — and spirit — with optimal nourishment.

Many of these recipes reintroduce familiar foods in new contexts, and present new foods in traditional settings, containing equal parts of exotic and familiar tastes. But you'll also discover that *Banquet of Health* is a unique source of innovative recipes and cooking techniques as well as a state-of-science guide to food choices and preparations. Written with a spirit of pure cooking pleasure, this book is an adventure into a life-enhancing diet.

All over the world, people who live simple lifestyles survive remarkably well on diets rich in whole grains, vegetables, beans, legumes, fruits, and fish. There is also powerful evidence that these cultures have profoundly less catastrophic disease than we enlightened and highly technologized sophisticates.

While acknowledging that our fast-paced, polluted environment is a major factor in our health impairment and ability to be well, we also need to change the way we eat. Changing the environment requires a group effort, which in itself is a mammoth undertaking. But changing your diet only requires a simple decision by one person — you!

A Banquet of Health is a giant step away from empty calories, and a definitive move toward good health through eating: first, as a method for restoring the body's immune system to its ultimate level, and second, for maintaining a life of quality — full of energy and increased physical strength.

Ask yourself, "How often do I wake up feeling joyful? Vigorous? Alive?" Thirty years of scientific study have validated that diet and its impact on biological health is the primary cause of the lethargic, weary, and burnt-out feelings many Americans experience when they wake up each day. If this is how you begin your day, wouldn't you like to turn this condition around and enjoy clarity of thought and vigor from the moment you awaken each morning.

Establishing optimal health is the formula for making that change, and its simplest ingredient is a commitment to optimal eating patterns. This does *not* mean giving up food enjoyment. However, it does mean paying attention to what foods you eat and how they affect your ability to work, play, and compete.

How much does a previous snack or meal deter or enhance your ability to think, remember, analyze, and respond to the challenges you face in your environment? And what would it mean to you personally to feel good enough to handle what comes your way all day long? These were the very questions that Penny and I asked ourselves when we started our investigation into healthy eating more than 15 years ago.

At that time there was little consensus among physicians about the role of diet in an epidemic of cancer and heart disease raging through our country's population. Beyond weight concerns, there was little attention paid to the impact of fat-laden, nutrient-poor eating habits. My profession stubbornly ignored the connection between the dietary habits which lead to degenerative disease.

Fortunately, there is now emphatic recognition that diet is an essential factor in disease prevention and treatment. Besides long-term results with weight loss and control, dietary changes have helped our patients reduce the need for medications, surgery, and other medical procedures. As a matter of fact, even heart disease — when countered with a lowfat diet, exercise, meditation, and group support, is now reversible without surgery.

Though we treat a variety of medical disorders in the Block Medical Center, much of our work has focused on cancer treatment and prevention. Early in my medical training, breast cancer affected one in 19 American women. By the time I completed medical school, the incidence had grown to one in 15. Recent figures show the epidemic now affects one in eight women — and the rate is rising! Regardless of ill-founded claims to the contrary, diet remains *the* chief cause of this increase.

A simple dietary change like reducing fat intake, from the monstrously high levels of 40 to 50 percent of the contents of our meals to reasonable levels of 10 to 20 percent, would reduce breast cancer to one-fifth its present level. In countries like Thailand, El Salvador, and Japan, where fat intake is below 20 percent, the incidence of breast cancer is much lower than in countries like the United States, Sweden, and Canada.

New evidence indicates that nutritional intervention may also diminish side effects of some conventional therapies, including chemotherapy for cancer, and may actually enhance the effectiveness of these treatments. To omit nutritional considerations as part of any valuable therapy may not only adversely affect the quality of life, it may also reduce chances of survival.

Much of the advice and many of the recipes in this book are essential ingredients in the individualized nutritional plans I advise for my patients. These foods, included in a regimen of exercise and stress care, have helped patients fight against disease, and have noticeably raised the performance level of world-class athletes.

As an integral part of my medical practice, Penny counsels patients not only on stress care and the benefits of better nutrition, but also on the positive attitude so important for making such a transition. In *Banquet of Health* she not only gives you an informative look inside that process, but also shows you how the simple act of cooking can become an expression of love and commitment that is so necessary in these difficult times.

— *Keith I. Block, M.D.*

PREFACE: GUIDELINES FOR FOOD SELECTION

What basic rudiments and what dietary regimen guided the final selection of recipes and recommendations included in this book? The foundation of this book is a diet composed of traditional staples, the kind of satisfying, healthful foods which have supported human life through the millennia—whole grains, fresh vegetables, fish, fruits, seeds, and nuts. As you glance through the recipes, you might notice that many dishes combine basic items in unexpected ways, marrying ingredients from very different cultural cuisines, for example, incorporating miso in a zesty south-of-the-border black bean soup. Yet the results, according to a test group, were pleasing — in fact, truly delectable.

The basic ingredients used in this collection of recipes may look just like those that have simmered in pots since antiquity. Such classic dishes do find their way into many menus, but in addition, thanks to kitchen alchemy, basic food items can be combined and presented in new forms to satisfy the experimental contemporary palate. There is an infinite number of ways to compose pleasing dishes using simple, natural foods awaiting your discovery.

As to the selection of specific ingredients, there are three basic guidelines:

1. Use whole foods, foods which have not been robbed of their essentials, foods which are in a form as close as possible to their natural, unadulterated state.

2. Select locally grown and preferably organic produce whenever possible.

3. Eat foods appropriate to seasonal changes and the climate you live in.

The first guideline seems self-explanatory, but the second and third may need further clarification. In all probability, vegetables and fruits shipped from another hemisphere, or even six states away, have been picked long before they were ripe (or ready to be plucked), so they may have been deprived of the time needed to develop full flavor and nutrition. In addition, since such transported vegetables or fruits need to look fresh after their long voyage, they may have been sprayed or "chemically" preserved in some way, which means that you can ingest harmful chemicals with every bite of dinner. On the other hand, it is likely that foods cultivated in your locale will not only be fresher, but more appropriate for your body's needs than those from a totally different environment and climate.

ADAPTATION

Considerable evidence now exists that all of us, through a process of natural selection, have evolved in a way which necessitates a specific balance between us and our natural environments. This balance includes temperature, of course, but also the amount of light and darkness, quality and nature of the water, and, certainly, the kinds of foods we eat. For example, tropical fruits, which are cooling foods, are perfectly appropriate to the indigenous population of the tropics, but are not suitable for people living in temperate or frigid climates. Seal blubber is a fine and appropriate food for Eskimos, but is an absurd and dangerous food for people living near the equator.

Only 50 years ago, your produce selection would probably have been limited to in-season fruits and vegetables grown within 100 miles of your local grocery store. The foods available to you were those which could be cultivated in your climate or region. Moreover, your habitat generally conformed to the geographic profile your parents, grandparents, or great-grandparents came from. Swedes migrated to the northern United States, where the climate, topography, and general ecology were similar to Sweden. Few Swedes immigrated to Arizona or New Mexico. The same was true of Germans, Poles, etc. Central and South America were colonized primarily by Spaniards — most of whom came from the semi-tropical regions of southern Spain. Obviously, there were and are exceptions, but the rule applied in most cases. Therefore, equilibrium was maintained.

With the introduction of technology for processing and freezing foods, along with jet transport, these patterns changed. Very rapidly, dietary habits became archaic and chaotic. Now we have the first clear indications that unless natural selection produces human beings capable of eating the flora and fauna of any form and kind, disequilibrium exists with all of its consequences.

Moreover, it is now dramatically evident that there is no such thing as a single nutritional regimen for 12 months of the year. With the exception of those areas where the climate remains essentially the same all year long and the food has a 12-month growth pattern, there must be a dietary adjustment to each season — fall, winter, spring, and summer. Even in the case of whole grains, there are clear variations. It is not an accident that rye is the grain of choice in the Scandinavian countries, particularly during the damp cold seasons, as compared to corn and wheat in the southern European countries. People adapt to the food that is most efficiently grown in their region, particularly since it provides for their needs most efficiently. Pineapples and coconuts are simply not appropriate to the residents of climatic areas in which these foods could not be grown, such as areas that include Alaska and Greenland.

Most of us already "know" these principles, but simply do not "know that we know." A great deal of seasonal dietary adjustments happens without any conscious deliberation. For instance, when the temperature soars above the 80-degree mark, most of us almost automatically tend to abandon long-cooked or hot-oven preparations like braised dishes or slow-simmered stews in favor of lighter fare, requiring less time in front of hot burners. On the hottest day of summer, gently steamed or quickly blanched vegetables, or crisp, cool, fresh salads possibly tossed with grains help to cool the body. Conversely, when the temperature plummets below freezing and we brace ourselves to walk outdoors, it makes no sense to fill up on cooling foods such as chilled juices, iced confections, cold raw salads, or refrigerated fruits. But a rich baked puree of hearty root vegetables can aid the body's adjustment to a January deep freeze. What we choose to eat, as well as how we prepare it, can translate into an easy adaptation to our immediate environment or a stressful adjustment, one which places an extra burden on our bodies' own internal mechanisms to re-establish equilibrium.

THE QUESTION OF NUTRITIONAL ADEQUACY

Be assured — Include a variety of the foods suggested in these recipes and your nutritional needs will be satisfied very comfortably. Two independent university dietitians evaluated the Block Nutritional Program®, developed by my husband, Keith I. Block, M.D., — the principles of which resulted in this book — and verified that following this food plan supplies adequate and better levels of all essential nutrients on a daily basis. In fact, several of Dr. Block's healthy patients who follow the dietary program and have kept careful records of their intake for a full week actually exceeded the Recommended Daily Allowances (RDAs) for several nutrients, including potassium, iron, vitamin A, vitamin B-12, thiamine, niacin, magnesium, protein, vitamin C, calcium, all amino acids, and manganese. It is noteworthy that these results were achieved on a dietary program which is completely free of red meat, poultry, and milk products. Moreover, these same patients were well within or slightly above the ideal ranges for intake levels of copper, sodium, zinc, riboflavin, and vitamin B-6. A number of nutrient values, such as those for selenium and folic acid — actually high in this program — are found in abundance in certain foods, such as sea vegetables and less familiar soy products, which have not been assayed in the usual nutritional listings. For certain people, such as those suffering from specific chronic or neoplastic disorders, or undergoing certain medical treatments, Dr. Block advises individual dietary programs in order to meet the unique nutritional requirements which are the consequences of those disease processes.

INTRODUCTION

"Food, glorious food. . . ." It is this famous refrain from *Oliver* which I have hummed as "my song" since discovering the tantalizing flavors, aromas, and textures that can be served up in the kitchen. Chewy oatmeal cookies laced with cinnamon and dotted with plump raisins, ribbons of smooth noodles floating in belly-warming, savory broths; in fact, all the magic produced on the stove or in the oven are like a childhood rhapsody to me. Thinking about food never conjured notions of measurable nutrients for me — that is, until recently. Food has always meant many-layered pleasure, from the basic physiologic satisfaction of feeling nourished, to simple sensory delights like the heady aroma of vanilla or a mouth filled with creamy sweetness, to more complex psychological dimensions of enjoyment, like personal, emotional associations with specific foods.

The pure experience of pleasure when first biting into any sweet or savory treat might not be measurable, and may seem irrelevant when considering health. Surprisingly, such experiences are important to body chemistry. The anticipation of enjoyment actually readies the gastro-intestinal tract, enabling digestive mechanisms to do a better job and absorb a larger quantity of nutrients. Pleasure and health *do* go together, even in this fundamental, physiological way. Scientific documentation about the effects of food on the body focuses almost exclusively on micronutrients and chemical properties, overlooking one of the most important criteria of our food choices — personal pleasure. That's an unwise omission. The whole person, not just the intellect, must be willing to adopt healthy eating habits. The opening portion of this book, which explains why some foods are recommended while others are to be avoided, might at first sound like a betrayal to true food lovers. Fortunately, that notion is incorrect. I love eating — all kinds of food! Yet, I eat with the comfortable awareness that the food which I put in my mouth will not injure my body chemistry — only strengthen it.

Eating well to satisfy health criteria should never prevent anyone from eating well to please the palate. All recipes included in this book brought pleasure to someone at sometime, and not a sense of deprivation. Simultaneously, these foods build the body's immune system, offer protection against a number of the most devastating diseases, and even help to correct some disabling disorders. Eating right provides energy-efficient fuel, enabling us to function in our demanding schedules with greater endurance, and to feel better on a day-to-day basis by helping to reduce the frequency and intensity of the little aches and pains of "no consequence" which chronically interfere with what we need to accomplish.

All of this suggests that it's time to discard the cliché, "If it tastes good, it must be bad for me." There's no need to be ascetic simply because we have become conscious of the whys and wherefores of nutrition. In fact, feeling deprived is the surest guarantee of not being able to stay with important dietary recommendations. A critical link exists between enjoying what we eat and a hearty appetite for living.

What kind of foods am I talking about? Not the gimmicky "health food" lists of do's and don'ts. Instead, what appears in these recipes are basic staples — in most cases in a form close to their whole, natural state — which have nourished humankind through the ages. In the company of varied seasonings, and partnered with other basic staples, many ancient types of food truly seem new, fresh, and unusual.

I invite you to experiment with the ideas suggested in this book. Use any of the recipes presented here as a springboard for your own ingenuity, and hunt down those preparations and special dishes to which your taste buds respond enthusiastically.

These recipes cover a wide range in terms of preparation: from simple (steamed vegetable dishes) to complex (almond cream-filled pastry puffs), and also represent many different cultural influences. Yet all are congruent with the basic guidelines of the Block Nutrition Program* and fundamental principles of healthy nutrition.

I won't pretend it's a simple task to transform your kitchen. But please don't get discouraged. It might take flexibility, perseverance, and patience, but your efforts will pay off. To illustrate this point, the difficulty but dividends of changing the way we eat, I can offer an endless assortment of anecdotes — my story, my friend's story, the story of the cousin of my good friend. But I'll just tell you mine. One Sunday afternoon, approximately 15 years ago, while I was alone with my two eldest daughters, then aged 8 and 4, I announced that I was going to prepare something very special for dinner — an entire meal using only the most "healthful" ingredients. I was no stranger to experimentation with different foods, in fact, I considered it fun. My guide in this new territory was an older macrobiotic* sourcebook with recipes and explanations of dietary principles. I began very confidently. Three hours later, with pots and pans precariously balanced on every inch of counter and my stove encrusted with spill-overs, I tasted my first spoonful. It was dreadful! Three thumbs down. All that work, all that anticipation, and I couldn't stand what I was tasting! And this was to be the way I would eat for the rest of my days? Inconceivable. I recall slumping down on the floor and teetering between tears and laughter. Fortunately, laughter won out. It was so outrageous, as if the wildest comedy sketch had been staged in front of my refrigerator. What I remember visualizing was an immense dumpster parked alongside my home, prepared to haul away my entire kitchen. (I didn't want to face clean-up, much less a second similar cooking attempt.) My kitchen, always friendly territory, suddenly seemed like some hostile, foreign realm.

Fortunately, no dumpster was available, and I was determined not to forego the pleasures of eating. Nor would I be daunted by this new "frontier." I bolstered my resolve and decided to try one new preparation each day. While commuting to a city college where I taught English at the time, I routinely planned the next day's meals, which had to include something never before attempted. I won't lie; it was a struggle. However, within a month I had developed a small repertoire of dishes which started to please me, and which were manageable in my kitchen, and in my time frame.

I discovered there is no one way to cook, no single formula for any dish. It's easy to vary a basic pot of rice by introducing new or favorite seasonings. Or, if the rice doesn't seem chewy enough to please, adjusting the quantity of liquid to produce the desired consistency. As long as the ingredients you use meet nutritional needs and their quality will not create chemical havoc in your body, your only limitations are what your palate dictates. Stated simply, the only right way is the one which tastes right to you. (However, don't be surprised if your tastes change as you discover the pleasure of whole, fresh foods no longer disguised by complicated sauces and seasonings.)

THE BASIC WHYS

Excess, not deficiency, is the primary cause of diet-linked disease in modern society. While too little food for our ancestors often meant inadequate protein and insufficient calories, our more ample food supplies and current eating habits do not represent benign abundance. Two to four times as much fat as our bodies are equipped to safely handle figures into three daily meals and in-between snacks — drizzled over popcorn, spread thickly over bread slices, spilled into a skillet for a quick sauté or fry. The quantity of fats we consume accumulates rapidly without conscious calculation. It multiplies because of easy access to ready, prepared foods, and adds up to clogged arteries, an overworked heart, and other chronic and debilitating illnesses. Similar problems result from refined sugars and sodium — abundantly available in all our foodstuffs — for which we have developed a hazardous preference.

For most adults, this information is neither new nor startling. Our daily newspapers and broadcast media communicate ominous messages regularly about the very real dangers in our eating habits. The happy consequence of this blitz of dietary warnings is a new attentiveness to the foods we choose. A more cautious intake of fat-laden foods, such as a dramatic reduction in red meat consumption; a cutback in sodium intake, such as removing the salt shaker from the dinner table; and refraining from additional sugar on breakfast cereal all represent intelligent steps toward a healthier physiology. Perhaps it is this new conscientious attitude — the result of our desire to not only live longer but to *live better,* to function better, and to feel better consistently — which prompted you to pick up this book.

FOODS TO AVOID
ANIMAL FOODS AND EXCESS PROTEIN

Excessive amounts of saturated fats and cholesterol are abundant in animal foods and dairy products like beef and butter. Besides the connection between fats and heart or vascular disorders, there is worldwide epidemiological evidence linking lipids (the generic name for fats and oils) with several forms of cancer, particularly breast, bladder, and colon-rectal. Colon-rectal cancer, for example, is one of the most common cancers in the United States. According to breakthrough research done by Dr. J. P. Cruse and his associates at the University College Hospital Medical School in London, later substantiated by parallel studies, fat consumption has been spotlighted as a primary promoter of this type of cancer. More recent evidence, a study conducted on 88,751 women by Dr. Walter C. Willett at Women's Hospital in Boston, reveals that those who eat red meat daily double their chances of getting colon cancer compared with non-meat eaters. For the group of women who ate meat more frequently than once per month, but less often than once per week, the risk of colon cancer was still 40 percent higher than for those who ate no meat, as reported in the December 13, 1990 *Chicago Tribune.*

In studying different population groups, scientists have found the highest incidence of colon cancer in those countries with the highest per capita meat consumption, such as, the U. S., Canada, Scotland, and New Zealand. In Japan, where traditionally there has been little fat intake, bowel cancer occurs less than one-third as frequently as in the U. S. (See following table, indicating breast cancer statistics as well). However, surveys indicate that when Japanese migrate to the United States and adopt a modern, Western diet with its heavy reliance on meat and dairy products, they experience a colon cancer incidence like that of other Americans.

NATIONAL CANCER RATE			
CANCER SITE		DEATH RATE PER 100,000 POPULATION	
		United States	Japan
Intestine	Males	17.2	4.6
	Females	19.3	5.0
Breast	Females	29.6	5.4
(Source: World Health Organization, 1973)			

Besides potentially hazardous quantities of fats, animal foods contain substantial levels of sodium. These naturally occurring salts in excessive amounts can contribute to hypertension and other cardiovascular disorders in "salt sensitive" individuals.

In our modern-day protein panic, each American annually consumes 193 pounds of red meat, 53 pounds of poultry, 294 eggs, and 375 pounds of dairy products (including cheese and other milk products). We are hooked on a protein-need myth, perpetuated in a significant part by the meat, dairy, and protein supplement industries. Actually, we may be consuming two to four times more protein than we require. This is another example of the faulty and dangerous assumption that "if some is good, then more is better."

Overindulging in animal protein can jeopardize our health. In a broad indictment of high protein intake, *U.S News and World Report* on May 20, 1991, quoted T. Colin Campbell, Professor of Biochemistry at Cornell University and one of the key researchers in the Cornell-China-Oxford study, referred to simply as "The China Study," as saying, "Excessive animal protein is at the core of many chronic diseases." As one example, high protein intake causes high levels of ammonia in the intestines. Dr. Willard Visek, Professor of Clinical Sciences at the University of Illinois Medical School, explains: "Ammonia behaves like chemicals that cause cancer or promote its growth. It kills cells...and it increases the mass of the lining of the intestines. What is intriguing is that within the colon the incidence of cancer parallels the concentration of ammonia." More recently, Campbell reported that "high protein intakes tend to decrease the cell-mediated immune response and tend to make one more susceptible to cancer." His recommendation, of course, is protein in moderation, achieved comfortably, for example, with the soy-based diets common in the less affluent regions of China.

Other experimental evidence suggests that consuming too much protein poses as great a risk factor in causing cancer as the consumption of fat per se. In one intriguing study conducted by McLean, Smith, and Driver in the professional journal *Carcinogenesis,* 1982, rats switched to a high-protein diet and exposed to a chemical carcinogen were beset by more tumors than those maintained on a low-protein diet while exposed to the same chemical carcingens.

It is now understood that excessive protein decreases the life span of certain cells, which can hasten the aging process. Moreover, due to the accumulation of urea, a byproduct of protein metabolism, too much protein can burden the kidneys. Since it is generally accepted that excess uric acid increases the incidence of joint inflammation, individuals with gout, arthritis, and other connective tissue problems should be cautioned to minimize animal proteins in their diets; and in fact, reduce the total amount of protein they eat, regardless of the source. Eating large quantities of protein also reduces the body's calcium levels, which affect the nervous, muscular, and skeletal systems. Examples of disorders linked with calcium loss are tetany (intermittent muscular spasms), cramping and fasciculations (involuntary muscle twitching), osteoporosis, and cardiac irregularities.

A BRIEF NOTE ABOUT CALCIUM

We appropriately concern ourselves about adequate calcium, but mistakenly persist in our meat and poultry eating habits while resorting to supplements as a possible remedy. Such dietary patterns render our best attempts to insure sufficient calcium ineffective, and, in fact, are completely counterproductive as long as we continue to eat large quantities of animal protein. Increasing calcium portions or daily capsules, even when significantly beyond the new RDAs, will not help win the calcium battle if still dining routinely on T-bone steaks, or even chicken. In effect, this dietary pattern is equivalent to betting on two different horses in the same race. Ingesting a mineral and the actual assimilation by the body of that mineral are two entirely separate and not necessarily cooperative processes. To increase real body reserves of calcium and to halt the leaching of this essential mineral from our bones, it is necessary to discontinue our modern-day habit of making meat or poultry the central item of our meals. Studies indicate that even with a very high calcium intake, when consuming as little as 75 grams of protein per day (on a standard American diet, many adults take in an excess of 100 grams of protein daily), more calcium is lost in the urine than is absorbed by the body, resulting in a negative calcium balance. Several ingestibles work against proper utilization of even the highest daily intake of calcium. Red meat, colas, and antacids actually suppress calcium absorption. Red meats and colas interefere with calcium assimilation due to their high level of phosphorus. Certain antacids, due to their aluminum content, cause excretion rather than absorption. We are thus left with a calcium deficit.

A landmark study indicates that our expectations about calcium intake are topsy-turvy. According to researcher T. Colin Campbell, in a comprehensive study conducted with Cornell University, Oxford University in England, and the Chinese Academies of Preventive Medicine and Medical Sciences, contrary to expectations, incidence of osteoporosis is actually highest among those populations who consume the most calcium, particularly among those whose major calcium source is protein-rich dairy products. In light of their findings, it is probable that our calcium needs are less than indicated by the RDAs, and very adequately met with vegetable-quality foods, such as dark leafy greens, grains, seeds, nuts, beans, and tofu, for example.

Even more data exist about the consequences of overindulging in protein. The evidence in the comprehensive study mentioned above, The China Project, argues convincingly that excess animal protein from any source can dramatically increase your potential for heart disease, as well as cancer. Studies conducted at the University of Western Ontario, reported in the May 20, 1991 issue of *U.S. News and World Report,* indicate that protein, independent of dietary fat, can elevate blood cholesterol levels.

Finally, before reaching for a second helping of veal chops, consider this fact: regardless of the food ingested, there are indications that excess eating can increase the number, size, and rapidity of tumor growth, an important issue if you are either harboring an undetected cancer or trying to block an already active one.

A NOTE ON THE USE OF OILS AND FATS

As a current marketing tactic, many food items are labeled "cholesterol free," implying that such products are free of hazardous fats. However, the absence of animal fats does not guarantee that vegetable oils are harmless. In truth, many vegetable oils — particularly those composed primarily of omega-6 fatty acids, such as safflower, sunflower, and corn oil — produce chemicals in the body like prostaglandin E2 and leukotrienes. With too much prostaglandin E2, disorders linked to chronic inflammation and immune deficiency are more likely. Omega-6 fatty acids have also been shown in laboratory tests to promote the growth of mammary tumors.

In contrast, omega-3 fatty acids, predominant in canola and flaxseed oils, pumpkin seeds, and walnuts, do not produce these adverse effects, and seem to inhibit the action of the omega-6 group. Therefore, canola oil is recommended over corn oil for healthier cooking. Even from the standpoint of cardiovascular health, the monunsaturate group — which includes canola and olive oil — seems to be the better choice.

Regardless of the quality or type of oil, oil means fat, and an excess quantity in the foods we eat imperils our health. High fat intake has been linked with cancers of the colon, prostate, and breast, and, of course, heart disease, which still kills more adults in the U.S. than all other causes of death combined. Most adult Americans consume 40 to 50 percent of their total calories in the form of fats. The mammoth China survey indicates that reducing dietary fat to 30 percent of calories consumed may not be low enough to ward off heart disease and cancer. The ideal percentage of dietary fat in terms of long-term health is not 25 to 30 percent of total calorie intake, but significantly lower — possibly somewhere in the range of 12 to 18 percent.

For the dramatic reversal of arterial blockage that Dean Ornish, M.D. and his colleagues witnessed, dietary fat was carefully maintained at a very low 10 percent. Ornish had discovered that there was no measurable or significant improvement for cardiovascular patients who reduced their fat consumption from 30 to 20 percent. In light of this, menus at the University of California, where the research originated, were designed with no more than 10 percent fat.

DAIRY PRODUCTS

Enticing billboards and persuasive television announcements, financed by the powerful dairy industry, lure us into believing the myth that milk is "pure and wholesome." Its fresh, white appearance is deceiving. Even after processing, milk is still not free of contaminants. An investigation by Consumers Union, published in the January 1974 issue of *Consumer Reports,* discovered bacterial counts exceeding 130,000 per milliliter in seven test samples of pasteurized milk, although government standards declare safe limits for consumption at a maximum of 20,000 bacteria per milliliter (about 1/5 teaspoon). In fact, one sample contained as many as 3,000,000 bacteria per ml, and a few contained numbers too large to measure accurately. More recent examination of milk samples reveals that a serious problem of contamination can reoccur.

In addition, the *Consumer Reports* study revealed that 21 out of 25 tested milk brands were contaminated with pesticides. Health officials concur there is no level of pesticides in milk that can be judged safe. Residues of chlorinated hydrocarbons were also detected in 21 of the milk samples analyzed. As these hydrocarbons accumulate in the body, they are not only capable of producing genetic mutations that can result in birth defects, but also have the potential of forming malignancies.

Added to this list of reasons to hesitate before consuming more dairy products is the possibility that the cow milked for a glass of milk or a slice of cheese might have been infected with a bovine C-type virus. In laboratory experiments, this virus produced leukemia in test animals.

Antibiotic residues in milk products pose a general health threat, but are also a particular problem for sensitive individuals, and can even provoke life-threatening allergic reactions. *(Siddique, I. H.)* For instance, scant quantities of penicillin in milk can produce not only irritating hives, but potentially fatal respiratory reactions. The widespread use of antibiotics — penicillin, tetracycline, streptomycin, neomycin, polymyxin, and others — introduced to eliminate bovine illnesses, has boomeranged, resulting in an indomitable strain of microorganisms which progressively become resistant to drug therapy. Another related concern is that by ingesting even very small amounts of antibiotics in milk on a day-to-day basis, we might blunt their effectiveness in countering serious bacterial infection.

Still other drugs, such as those in the sulfa group like sulfamethazine, are suspected carcinogens. An FDA survey of March, 1988 discovered traces of sulfamethazine in 74 percent of milk samples from various sources. In response, FDA officials attempted to stop dairy farmers from using drugs which could prove harmful to milk consumers. Yet, even in December, 1989, *The Wall Street Journal* reported finding antibiotic and sulfa residues in 38 percent of the milk tested in their own survey. Only two out of the 30 drugs actually present in milk can even be detected by conventional FDA laboratory tests.

As more evidence accumulates, explains Frank A. Oski, M.D. in his book *Don't Drink Your Milk* (Mollica Press, 1983), we begin to realize that milk and milk products are not the benign foods we believe them to be. Between 18 months and 4 years of age, most people begin to lose lactase activity, an intestinal enzyme action that breaks down lactose, the natural sugar present in milk. Without sufficient lactase, even preschoolers, older siblings, and, of course, parents can experience painful gastrointestinal symptoms — abdominal cramping, distention, and diarrhea — in digesting milk or foods derived from milk. Since this decline in lactase is a normal process of maturing, perhaps it was never nature's intention for us to drink milk or eat foods with lactose after the weaning age.

Investigating the possible hazards of milk, like opening Pandora's box, reveals the curious fact that it is not just the milk itself (whether whole milk, low fat, or skimmed) which can prove injurious to our bodies, but homogenization, which just might jeopardize our health. Kurt M. Oster, M.D., Emeritus Chief of Cardiology at Park City Hospital in New York, and Donald J. Ross, Ph.D. in Biochemistry, have done intriguing research on this issue. In *The XO Factor* (Park City Press, 1983), they report that homogenization — a procedure which emulsifies fat droplets and alters milk so the creamier portion does not separate — unfastens the xanthine oxidase (XO) enzyme, allowing it to travel past the intestinal walls and into the bloodstream, potentially producing lesions and plaquing in the artery walls, and predisposing young children and adults to grave medical problems. Acording to Oster's reports, damage from the XO enzyme can be subtle but cumulative, and particularly insidious because it is invisible and often undetected until serious irreversible symptoms develop. Ironically, while we insist that our school-age children drink their milk — homogenized milk — we might inadvertently be abetting the plaquing and congestion of their young blood vessels, leaving them vulnerable to subsequent athero-sclerosis and its devastating consequences.

REFINED CARBOHYDRATES AND SUGAR

Refined carbohydrates and processed foods have been found guilty of causing many modern-day health concerns. One obvious and visible consequence of consuming refined simple sugars is tooth decay. Half of all 55 year-olds in this country lose their teeth due, primarily, to cavities and gum disease. But the hazards of refined simple sugar are even more extensive. These sugars require minerals and vitamins to metabolize them. Since such sugars are nutritionally empty, they rob the body of the B-complex vitamins, pyridoxine, pantothenic acid, and folate, nutrients which sustain our immune system functions. It is not surprising that experiments suggest that our sugar habit can seriously reduce our immune capacity, thereby multiplying the risk of infectious disease.

Our sugar habit can also play an active role in promoting such disorders as hyperactivity and diabetes, place a heavy burden on the pancreas, and create a susceptibility to ulcers and heart disease. Satisfying our craving for sweets can exact a high price on the body's trace minerals. Specifically, refined simple sugar steals chromium, necessary for regulating blood sugar and helpful in fending off diabetes (*Longevity,* February, 1991). In contrast to refined carbohydrates and simple sugars, chromium is plentiful in whole grains, leafy green vegetables, and fruits. Moreover, according to research conducted by Dr. K. R. Scragg and his colleagues (*British Medical Journal*, 288:1113, 1984), refined sugar in soft drinks and desserts increases the risk of developing gallstones. Peptic ulcers may be more the consequence of heavy sugar consumption than the result of stress.

It's almost impossible to wander through grocery aisles and locate a can or package that does not include sugar. Sugar can be cleverly concealed on labels behind an alias of "sucrose" or "dextrose." Even corn syrup is just another refined sugar. Sixty-five percent of the sugar consumed comes packaged in processed foods, while only 35 percent of the sucrose in the American diet is actually sprinkled on at the table or added in the kitchen.

Although there is no physiological need for refined sugar, estimates are that ¼ of the total caloric intake for the average American is sugar. This percentage is even higher for children in the U.S., who consume almost half (48 percent) of their daily calories in the form of simple sugars. Although, in general, Americans have cut their consumption of table sugar to approximately 60 pounds per year, individual intake of caloric sweeteners, such as corn syrup and molasses, can easily add up to 150 pounds per year.

Despite these hazards, good health does not demand austerity or abstinence. Satisfying sweeteners are available, particularly grain sweeteners such as rice syrup and barley malt, which, when used in moderation, do not create havoc for the pancreas nor stress digestive organs. Because these grain sweeteners are primarily maltose, a more complex sugar than those that make up simple refined white or brown varieties, they metabolize in a more gradual manner and are less shocking to the digestive system. Foods like sweet vegetables, including winter squash, carrots, or sweet potatoes, and fruits in judicious quantities, can also be used to satisfy a craving for sweets without hazard.

CAUTION REGARDING THE NIGHTSHADE VEGETABLE GROUP:

As an additional condsideration, particularly for diabetics or for those with blood glucose problems, baked potatoes rank very high on the glycemic index, a scale which indicates how quickly a specific carbohydrate raises blood sugar. This means that a food like baked potatoes can cause an unforeseen and rapid rise in blood sugar, while foods low on the glycemic index can calm rising blood sugar, and may even help to reduce cholesterol and triglyceride levels.

With certain digestive disorders or gastrointestinal complaints, tomatoes can be troublesome. Ulcer sufferers, for example, are properly cautioned to avoid tomatoes. In fact, perhaps anyone concerned about acid/alkaline balance should be somewhat wary of eating tomatoes. However, when tomatoes are incorporated into a dish, adding a judicious amount of salt modifies their acid content.

After this discussion of foods to avoid, it must be emphasized that cutting back and cutting out do not equal a total remedy to our dietary ills. There are certain foods with specific positive, salutary effects which must be introduced into our regular menus.

RECOMMENDED FOODS
WHOLE GRAINS

In travelling from the farmfield to the grocery shelf, processed and packaged grain products have been stripped of most vitamins and minerals. Robbed of nature's rich nutrients, these refined carbohydrates are loaded with artificial supplements. In contrast, whole grains are indeed "the real thing."

Professor Paul C. Mangelsdorf, in the July, 1963 issue of *Scientific American,* made this definitive statement: "Cereal grains... represent a five-in-one food supply which contains carbohydrates, proteins, fats, minerals, and vitamins. A whole grain cereal, if its food values are not destroyed by the over-refinement of modern processing methods, comes closer than any other plant product to providing an adequate diet."

Whole grains heal the body as well as fuel it. High fiber, the stuff of cereal grains, reduces the risk of colon and other cancers. As a bonus, whole grains produce a beneficial form of cholesterol — high density lipoproteins (HDLs). Unlike the harmful type of cholesterol associated with animal foods (LDLs), this favorable cholesterol actually breaks down dangerous saturated fat and oil residue and assists in the prevention of arterial plaquing.

Perhaps the most impressive role whole grains can play is in strengthening the immune system. The May, 1980 issue of the *Hospital Tribune* reported that diseases stemming from a weak immune system "are associated with a high incidence of malignancies." Three vitamins in particular are essential to immunity: pyridoxine (vitamin B6), folic acid, and pantothenic acid. All are plentiful in whole grains. According to Dr. A. E. Axelrod of Pittsburgh University Medical School, if any one of these three is absent from the diet, the body cannot manufacture antibodies (proteins that fight disease). Unfortunately, these three elements of the B complex are left on the milling room floor in the refining process. Therefore, they are not present in white bread, white flour products, white rice, or degerminated cornmeal. The implications of this are tremendous; a natural, whole grain diet can build resistance to disease, while a refined foods diet cannot.

Whole cereal grains have supported life in every culture around the globe for millenia. In fact, the word "cereal" derives from the same root as *Ceres,* the goddess of agriculture in the Roman Pantheon, suggesting the lofty stature of grains in antiquity. For 10,000 years, grains have been cultivated as the principal food item on which all humanity has subsisted, with legumes, vegetables, seeds, fruits, nuts, and even animal foods, serving more as an accompaniment than as the primary fare of the meal. Grains traditionally would not have been labeled as the "starch side dish" in a dinner, but as *the* dinner. Only during this century, particularly in Western society, has the status of grains diminished and their actual value depreciated.

When whole, each grain of cereal is both the seed and fruit of the grass plant. All of the essential elements necessary to generate an entire new cycle of life are contained within one tiny, unmilled grain. The milling process shatters the kernal, exposing valuable nutrients to oxidation and vitamin loss. Moreover, refined flour has been robbed of 80 percent of its nutritional value. For example, gone from denuded wheat is a wealth of vitamins, minerals, fiber, and a huge proportion of usable protein once the essential amino acid lysine is removed. Only a small percentage of total foods consumed today are from whole grains, and these often appear in the most nutritionally depleted form, that is, stripped, bleached, sifted, sugar-sweetened, and fat-laden.

Although all types of grain — rice, barley, millet, wheat, oats, rye, corn, buckwheat, quinoa, and teff, for example — are members of the same botanical family and are nutritional cousins, they are not interchangeable in terms of culinary characteristics or physiological effect.

RICE

Currently the world's third leading food crop, rice is the primary nourishment for more than 1.5 billion people, which represents more than 50 percent of the world's population. In the typical American menu, however, rice plays only a bit part and, at best, is peripheral to the "real meal." Unfortunately, the form of this grain which is most familiar in the U. S., and customary even to those who subsist on rice, is the white, polished variety. All unrefined rice, meaning rice with only the husk removed, is referred to as "brown," although it is really a pale tan in color. By removing the outer layers — the bran and germ — of the rice and polishing the white inner grain, what remains is seriously deficient in B vitamins and minerals. Eighty percent of the thiamine (vitamin B1) is absent in white rice, which in a rice-dependent culture can lead to Beri-Beri and a degeneration of the nervous system; 60 percent of the iron and 70 percent of the niacin have been removed; plus its significant fiber content is missing. Recent studies by the United States Department of Agriculture show rice bran's fiber is effective in reducing dangerous levels of cholesterol.

Rice dates back 5,000 years to cultivation in India. Its use travelled, along with the spread of Buddhism, to the Orient where rice became the mainstay of the diet, comprising more than 50 percent of everything eaten. In its polished form, white rice was first introduced by Confucius. Because of expensive processing, it became a symbol of affluence, originally favored by the aristocracy, but eventually preferred by the larger population, much to their nutritional detriment.

Although over 7,000 varieties exist, rice is usually categorized in three groups: long grain, short grain, and medium grain. When cooked, the grains of the long variety are light, fluffy, and separate which makes long grain an excellent selection for pilafs and light summer salads. Short grain is somewhat higher in trace minerals and starch, and when cooked, individual grains are more plump and moist. Short grain rice tends to stick together, producing a hardier side-dish, which can be satisfying unadorned, with a simple condiment, or suitable for croquettes, patties, or rice rolls. Short grain also combines well with chestnuts, wheat berries, aduki beans, and onions, as examples. Medium grain, as its name implies, is somewhere between the long and short types in its size, texture, and cooking characteristics. Another category of rice, usually distinguished from the three types used for daily fare, is sweet rice, sometimes referred to as "sticky rice" because of its glutinous consistency. Sweet rice works well in puddings, in a confection called *amasake*, and in a puffed, chewy preparation called *mochi*.

What is referred to as *wild rice* is actually not a variety of rice but a type of aquatic grass seed native to North America. Although very expensive, wild rice swells considerably in cooking and can actually increase fourfold in volume. A nutrient-rich grain, it has a distinctive full, nutty flavor and chewy texture. Using a small proportion of wild rice as a pleasing contrast in a grain dish, or alone as special party fare, makes it an interesting menu option.

BARLEY

One of the oldest cultivated grains, barley was once used as a form of currency in the ancient Near East, and represented the basic standard for measurement in the Sumerian system. Barley still serves as a primary food in Tibet, but it is rarely even a menu entry in the U. S. Barley is customarily used in the U. S. for beer production and livestock feed.

Easier to digest than wheat, barley was viewed in ancient lore as valuable to eliminate accumulated fats and salts from an excess of animal foods, and was said to stimulate the liver and lymphatic system, thus accelerating waste discharge. Current research validates much of this folk wisdom. In studies done at the University of Wisconsin (*American Health,* May, 1985), two properties of barley which actually block cholesterol production in the liver were identified by chemist Asaf Qureshi and his colleagues.

Barley has merited the reputation of being a very filling and soothing grain. It is frequently included as a secondary item in a vegetable soup or stew. Yet barley works just as effectively as the main ingredient, for example, in a side dish accompanied by sauteed mushrooms and onions, or featured in a grain salad.

MILLET

Millet's use dates further back in antiquity than any other grain, and even today is the staple fare for one-third of the world's population. This grain is one of the hardiest and survives even in arid climates, unlike other grains in the grass family. Yet in this country, millet is commonly recognized only as bird seed. Millet has the capacity to grow in conditions which are poorly suited for most grains, such as sandy soil and little moisture, making its cultivation possible even in the dry, hot regions of Africa, the Middle East, and Asia.

The only alkaline-forming grain, millet is easy on the digestive system and is helpful with an acid condition or gastrointestinal inflammation. Nutritionally, it is 200 to 300 percent higher in iron than other grains and contains all but one of the essential amino acids. A small, mild grain with a subtle nutty flavor, millet can be prepared like rice and served by itself or with gravy, as a patty, or in breads and muffins. Because it tends to become dry as it cools, millet is often accompanied by a sauce or gravy.

WHEAT

Although wheat is not native to the American continents, and in fact, was transported to our soil by Columbus, it now represents the major U. S. cash crop. Wheat is cultivated and consumed more widely around the globe than any other food, and for this reason, as well as its inherent nutritional value, has earned the designation "the staff of life." The whole wheat berry, as the whole grain is called, is nutrient rich — not only an excellent complex carbohydrate but high in B vitamins, trace minerals like magnesium (necessary for calcium utilization) and zinc — as well as a good quality protein. Although wheat protein is deficient in two amino acids, lysine and tryptophan, these can be supplied by eating the wheat with a complementary food such as legumes. The only significant nutrients lacking in the whole wheat berry are vitamins A, B12, C, and one mineral — iodine. A whole wheat berry can retain its freshness for several years, but once ground into flour, it rapidly becomes susceptible to rancidity. It is advisable to use wheat flour immediately after grinding, or refrigerate or freeze it.

Americans consume about 128 pounds of wheat or wheat flour per person annually, but usually in its least nourishing, processed forms. The most familiar form in which wheat is eaten, of course, is bread prepared using flour from hard spring wheat. Spring wheat, planted during the spring season, usually in colder, northern climates, and harvested in the fall, contains a higher protein or gluten level than winter wheat, which is planted during the fall months, harvested during the following spring, and contains proportionately more starch and less gluten. It is the sticky gluten, or wheat protein, that helps yeasted dough to rise. Each category of wheat is also designated as either "hard" or "soft," depending on its relative gluten or starch content. "Hard" signifies a higher gluten content, making it preferable for breads and seitan (often called "wheat meat"). "Soft" indicates more starch. For this reason, most pastry flours are produced from the soft, winter wheat berry. Another wheat classification, durum wheat, contains almost no gluten or protein and is used as flour primarily in noodles. Semolina appearing on a label indicates the refined derivative of durum wheat.

Three other forms of processed wheat can appear in breakfast, lunch, or dinner preparations: bulgur, cracked wheat, and couscous. Bulgur is made from wheat berries which are partially boiled, dried, and broken into smaller pieces. Since it has been parboiled, bulgur does not require further cooking, only the addition of boiling water or stock and soaking time. For this reason, bulgur can be very quickly and conveniently used in salads, pilafs, and stuffings. Bulgur usually retains the bran, but can go rancid, so it requires immediate use or refrigerated storage. Cracked wheat has not been parboiled, but has been partly milled. It has a lighter color and flavor than bulgur, but is not as nutritionally complete. The couscous most often available in this country is steamed, dried, toasted semolina, akin to pasta and has undergone similar processing. It fares well in soups, salads, stews (for example, with chickpeas and vegetables), and even in desserts.

OATS

Originally regarded as a troublesome weed which encroached on cultivated barley and wheat crops, oats eventually became standard fare in northern Europe, England, and Ireland. In Scotland, oats became a true mainstay of the diet, appearing in a variety of dishes besides the familiar porridge. This grain has the capacity to withstand cold, damp climates and thrive where less hardy grains have perished. In fact, oats have been found growing wild all the way from the British Isles to eastern Europe.

Nutritionally, oats provide a bonus to any meal plan. This grain has a richer protein content than wheat, contains the highest percentage of poly-unsaturated fats of any cultivated grain, and, for this reason, is believed to impart warmth and stamina. During the 19th century, Scottish universities are said to have observed "Oatmeal Monday," when thrifty parents would arrive with a hefty sack of oats to ensure nourishment for their children through the brutal, chilling winters. Easily digested, oats also provide B vitamins, calcium, iron, and a much-touted cholesterol-trapping fiber. Oats also possess a natural antioxidant which helps oat flour retain its freshness and resist rancidity.

The most familiar forms of oats are groats, old-fashioned rolled, and steel cut oats. Groats, the whole oat kernels, are more tender than wheat berries and can be cooked by themselves as a breakfast dish, or prepared in stuffings, pilafs, soups, and casseroles. Because oats are a soft grain, once the inedible hull has been removed after steaming, they are easily flattened with giant steel rollers into old-fashioned rolled oats. In this form, oats have multiple uses in soups, cookies, and pie crusts, for example. Of course, rolled oats most commonly appear in breakfast bowls as the familiar oatmeal, a simple 10 to15 minute preparation. Steel cut oats, often called "Scotch oats," are made from unrefined groats which are chopped into two or three pieces. The steel cut variety frequently is cooked as a slightly chewy break-fast dish, or is used in Scottish oat cakes and *cranachan*.

The good quality fat content of oats makes them ideal for creating a "creamy" consistency in soups and sauces. Thus, "cream" of mushroom soup can be made without introducing even an ounce of dairy products in the preparation. Given the range of possible oat preparations and the nutrient rich quality of oats, it is baffling that well over 90 percent of our total oat crop is used for animal feed, not human consumption.

RYE

Like oats, rye was at first regarded with contempt as a lowly weed and a spoiler of wheat crops. Gradually it acquired value and became an important crop in northern and eastern Europe, particularly because rye managed to survive the most unfavorable growing conditions, even sandy, infertile soil. Moreover, rye could grow in cold climates, tolerating only short, parched summers, in areas as far north as the Arctic Circle, and even thrived in dry, mountainous terrains or, curiously, under the opposite conditions — extreme, unremitting dampness. An additional agricultural advantage recommends rye grains — it can be planted repeatedly without risking soil depletion.

Rye has a higher calcium, vitamin B complex, and protein content than wheat. Of all the whole grains, rye has the highest percentage of the amino acid lysine, which is virtually absent in wheat. However, rye is proportionately low in gluten. Since gluten makes yeast rise, rye flour is usually combined with gluten-rich wheat flour. Because rye flour ferments rapidly, it is particularly suited to the making of sourdough loaves. Of all types of breads, sourdough rye is said to be the most "medicinal," that is, gentlest on the digestive system.

In northern Europe until the last few decades, rye bread was a staple food. Heavy rye cakes traditionally sustained Swedes during their long, cold winters. In Finland, rye commonly appeared in dried, crisp wheels of flatbread. Not actually a wheat substitute, rye has a decidedly more robust character and heartier flavor than wheat. Rye's most familiar role is in breads or crisp crackers. As a flour it can be used to produce either a sweet Swedish loaf or a slightly sour-tasting German rye bread. The rye bread popular in this country is a weak relative of the original, hearty, crusted European loaf, and actually contains only 5 to 10 percent rye flour, used in combination with white flour and caraway seeds. Only true pumpernickel bread is made almost exclusively from coarsely ground rye flour.

Besides being ground into flour, rye berries or groats can be soaked whole, cooked, and used in casseroles such as a lentil-rye dish. Rolled rye, like other rolled grains, can be used in breakfast dishes. Even rye grits, whole rye cracked into six or seven pieces, make a substantial, hot breakfast dish and an interesting addition to breads.

CORN

A genuine American native, corn was found growing in what is now Cuba by Columbus and his crew approximately 500 years ago. Evidence of corn's presence in the Americas reaches back to ancient, even prehistoric, times. Corn cobs approximately 5,600 years old have been discovered in New

Mexico, and actual grains of corn pollen, possibly 80,000 years old, were located near Mexico City. In its many hues (red, yellow, blue, white, and striped) and sizes, corn represented basic nourishment to the Inca and Mayan people. In the mythology of these societies, corn was revered as a true deity and life-source, a "child of the sun god."

Corn is the one grain originally cultivated in the Americas and agriculturally bred by Native Americans to adapt almost miraculously to climatic conditions from the southernmost point of South America all the way to Canada. The American colonists chose to cultivate corn instead of wheat because it was easier to grow and prepare. Corn is currently the most important crop in the U. S., although almost 90 percent of all corn harvested ends up as livestock feed rather than on our dinner plates.

If not degerminated, corn has a protein pattern similar to that of wheat; neither tryptophan nor lysine is present. However, accompanying legumes with corn supplies these amino acids easily. Traditional processing of corn — soaking kernels in fire ash and water and then grinding on a soft limestone metate — enhances corn's iron content by 37 percent and its calcium content by an astonishing 2,000 percent. In fact, some nutritionists report that stone-ground and lime-softened corn tortillas contain the most perfect ratio of calcium, phosphorus, and magnesium of all foods.

Each type of corn — soft corn, sweet corn, popcorn, flint, and dent — produces unique dishes: simple popcorn snacks, corn chowder, corn puddings, cornbreads, hoecakes, and polenta, to name a few. Soft corn is used primarily for flour, the yellow variety having a higher level of beta carotene than the white. Sweet corn, an American favorite as "corn on the cob," has the least starch but highest sugar content, while popcorn is highest in starch content.

BUCKWHEAT

Buckwheat belongs more to the botanical category of fruits than grains, related more to the rhubarb and dock families than to wheat. Not actually a grain, buckwheat shares many nutritional attributes of the grain family, though nutritionally richer than most true grains. With its high quality protein balance providing a protein value superior to any other plant, a rich iron concentration, a B vitamin level which is 200 percent greater than that of whole wheat, and significant calcium and potassium levels, buckwheat should be regarded as a nutritional superhero in the grain category of food items.

Buckwheat used to be important in American cuisine. It lost its prominence gradually after the turn of the century, much to our culinary and nutritional loss. In 1866, 20 times more buckwheat was grown in the United States than is currently cultivated. This hardy plant had been favored for its easy cultivation even in the least hospitable circumstances. It adapts to poor quality and rocky soils, and survives in very cool, damp climates. Moreover, buckwheat resists insect infestation and matures within 60 days. It is therefore not surprising that in the mountainous, western regions of China, buckwheat has been a staple food since prehistoric times. More recently, middle and eastern Europeans and Russians have enjoyed buckwheat primarily as a porridge, although buckwheat pancakes have been popular in Europe much as they have been in the U. S. during an earlier era. Of course, buckwheat flour appears as the star ingredient in the popular Russian blinis, delicate crêpe-like pancakes well-suited to dinner if stuffed with vegetables and a savory sauce, or prepared as an appealing and fortifying breakfast dish.

Buckwheat provides a meat-like stamina, and in effect, gives an insulation against the bitterly cold winters of the northern U.S., Europe, and Asia. With only the hard outer husk removed, the whole, unmilled buckwheat kernel or groat is surprisingly tender, cooks more quickly than millet, and is ready in one-fourth to one-half the time of brown rice. Buckwheat most commonly appears in two forms: roasted and unroasted. Roasting buckwheat imparts a bold, nutty flavor and a darker hue. Once roasted, whole buckwheat groats are called kasha. With its stronger flavor and aroma, kasha is well suited for use in fish or poultry stuffings, pilafs, and the traditional varnishkas, a hardy combination of pilaf and noodles. In its unroasted form, this grainlike fare, referred to simply as buckwheat, is easily paired with more delicately flavored foods, made into a hot, creamy cereal, and even used in salads.

QUINOA (keen-wa)

A newly rediscovered ancient grain, quinoa is a tiny ivory, almost translucent seed that was the primary nourishment for the great Inca civilization, reverently called the "mother grain." Some 3,000 years ago, quinoa enjoyed an exalted status; seen as sacred, it was central to the mysteries of Inca religious rituals. Quinoa was so venerated that to initiate each planting season, the supreme Incan ruler ceremoniously sowed the first seeds using a gold spade. At one point, three times as much quinoa was grown as corn, and its cultivation, dating back some 5,000 years, preceded corn considerably. For political reasons — to cripple the Inca civilization — as well as for agricultural and shipping factors (potatoes transport well and grow quickly and easily, while corn can grow more suitably in most European soil), Spanish conquistadors and subsequent missionaries attempted to terminate quinoa cultivation.

Yet quinoa was grown secretly, for the most part in mountainous terrains and at high altitudes which corn could not tolerate. Quinoa has remained a major protein source in the Andes, and with good reason. Surpassing other grains in its percentage of protein — 16.2 percent on average as compared to 7.5 percent for rice and 14 percent for wheat — quinoa also has a balance of amino acids which is superior to wheat. It is unusually rich in the essential amino acid lysine, frequently not available in vegetable proteins. Moreover, calcium in uncooked quinoa surpasses an equivalent quantity of cow's milk (actually one cup of cooked quinoa contains as much calcium as a quart of milk), and represents an excellent source of the vitamin B complex and vitamin E.

Short preparation time and menu adaptability also recommend quinoa for regular use. Cooked fully in just 12 to 15 minutes, quinoa is a boon to conscientious eaters on a harried schedule. With just a brief simmering, quinoa quadruples in size, producing a fluffy, light, non-sticking grain. And because its nutty flavor is delicate and not overbearing, it partners easily with many other ingredients as when gently simmered in a vegetable stew, a featured member of a salad, or in distinctive sweet or savory muffins. Although botanically not a true cereal grain, but the dried fruit of an herbal family which includes lamb's-quarters, quinoa is treated as a grain for our cooking purposes.

TEFF

Teff, the world's smallest grain, has been the premier food crop of the Abyssinians in the highlands of Ethiopia for thousands of years. So tiny that it takes 150 grains of teff to equal the weight of an individual grain of wheat, this remarkable food staple has earned the label of "supergrain" on the basis of its nutritional credentials and pleasing flavor. Nutritive-rich, whether the white, brown, or more uncommon red seed variety, 100 grams of teff boasts a calcium content of 172 milligrams (17 times the calcium of whole wheat or barley), approximately 76 milligrams of iron, and 10 grams of protein, as well as other vitamins and trace minerals. Difficult to harvest and not subsidized by the Ethiopian government, as is the case of more economically valued crops such as wheat, teff remains one of the world's most obscure grains. A moist, pancake-like flatbread called "injera" made simply of teff flour, pure water, and sea salt — no oil, milk, eggs, or wheat needed — is the traditional staple for the Abyssinian highlanders. This grain can be prepared in just 15 minutes for a tasty variation of hot breakfast cereal, surpassing oatmeal in nutrition.

BEANS (Legumes)

Beans are the perfect nutritional complement to grains, and the two have appeared together in almost every traditional cuisine around the globe. Because beans are an economical food, they have acquired a humble image which has been difficult to shake, making them unpopular in more prosperous times. During the Great Depression and the war-rationing years, they were pigeonholed as ideal budget stretchers or "fillers," a label implying that they wouldn't be anyone's first menu selection. Any lingering prejudice is unfortunate and misplaced as beans lend themselves to a wide range of delicious, satisfying preparations, offer ample health and nutritional bonuses, and are inexpensive. Since it is almost impossible to ruin their preparation, and since they require little attention, beans are a true friend to a busy cook. Even if "overcooked" an hour or more, they probably will not taste overdone. The earthy but mild character of beans, which does not overwhelm the taste buds, enables them to carry a range of other flavors. The simple addition of onions, garlic, and/or herbs can almost magically transform a modest pot of beans into a glamorous entrée. In this era of sophisticated palates and experimentation, it is reassuring to witness a new attitude materializing — beans are currently gaining gastronomical respect. Today, there is no need to expect disdain if you serve as the primary fare of a meal a steaming hot bowl of smooth red bean soup garnished with chopped scallions and cilantro, accompanied by a fresh, moist piece of corn bread, or a rich lentil pâté laced with just a hint of garlic, joined by a bulgur-cucumber-parsley vinaigrette.

Bean preparation is not an onerous task. The basic process involves putting a cup of beans in a pot with water and turning on the flame. Since most beans become more tender and digestible if presoaked, not a complicated procedure, it is generally advised. (Adukis, black-eyed peas, lentils, and split peas do not require presoaking, although it will not hurt them to do so.) To presoak beans, just before going to sleep at night, rinse the beans, then submerge them in cool water, and allow them to soak overnight. Or, bring rinsed beans to a boil in three to four times their volume of water, turn off the flame, cover, and let them soak for an hour. Before boiling or pressure-cooking presoaked beans, rinse then cook the beans in twice their volume of water without salt. (Salt or salty ingredients should not be added to beans until they are tender, as salt toughens their skins and increases the cooking time.) The notorious intestinal "back-talk" associated with beans is caused by oligosaccharides, a natural componenet of precooked beans, but these can be broken down and flatulence avoided with presoaking and proper cooking. A four-inch ribbon of *kombu*, a sea vegetable belonging to the *Laminaria* group, added to the cooking pot for each cup of beans will enhance their mineral content and make them more digestible.

Some people might initially experience digestive discomfort from eating beans. Often it takes moderation and a gradual dietary shift to allow our digestive systems to undergo an adjustment period. Switching abruptly from a primarily non-fibrous, meat-based diet to one containing 40 grams or more of fiber per day can potentially create havoc in the intestinal tract. Instead, starting with a ½-cup serving of beans per day and gradually increasing this amount, not exceeding 1 cup, will make this dietary transition less troublesome.

Beans are a nutritional asset in any meal. They are low in calories and fats (cooked beans are approximately 2 percent fat, while red meat and hard cheese can be anywhere from 50 to 60 percent fat), yet high in protein (14 to 20 grams in one cup), fiber, the B complex and other vitamins, and essential minerals such as calcium, magnesium, iron (½ cup of kidney beans provides the same quantity of iron as 6 ounces of lean red meat), phosphorus, potassium, and zinc. The legume group represents a smart shift from high-fat meats for getting necessary proteins.

Beyond the obvious nutritional value, research at the University of Kentucky, reported in the *Federation Proceedings Report*, November, 1985, suggests that beans can benefit diabetics since they reduce insulin requirements. In addition, protease inhibitors, a specific substance found in beans, have been demonstrated in numerous studies to curb the development of certain cancers, such as breast, colon, and prostate. According to radiobiologist Ann Kennedy, preliminary trials at Harvard University suggest that the Bowman-Birk group of protease inhibitors, which are not destroyed by heat or digestion, may possibly diminish the incidence of lung and liver cancer (*American Health*, July/August, 1988). There is even evidence that legume fiber reduces total blood cholesterol in two ways: it dissolves in water, forming a gel that binds with cholesterol which then passes out of the body; and it suppresses cholesterol production in the liver.

Yet none of these biochemical benefits alone could successfully market beans as a desirable food stuff if it weren't for the simple fact that beans can be delicious. There are so many kinds to choose from. The following represents only a partial listing:

Aduki (Adzuki, Azuki): A small, burgundy-red bean, the aduki is considered the most easily digested of the legumes. Since adukis are popular in the Orient, they are often seasoned with ginger, shoyu, or miso in soups or stews, but are equally as tasty in a grain salad or pilaf, for example, when combined with rice or bulgur.

Anasazi: The anasazi (a Navajo word meaning "ancient one"), cultivated for about nine centuries, has been a treasured staple in the American Southwest for several hundred years. Not surprising since this speckled bean is an excellent protein source, notably high in iron, phosphorus, and thiamine (2 ounces of dried beans provides one-fourth of the thiamine RDA), and a good provider of calcium, as well as other essential nutrients. In any dish commonly using pintos or kidneys, from full-bodied soups to refried beans or stews, the anasazi makes a delicious alternative.

Black Beans (Turtle Beans): Used in the popular classic black bean soup, in traditional Latin American favorite dsihes, and in the simple but perfect combination with rice, these flavorful beans play a favored role in Spanish and Mediterranean dishes as well. They unite successfully with strong flavors, especially onions, garlic, cumin, oregano, olive oil, and even lemon juice.

Black-Eyed Peas (Cowpeas): These quick-cooking, easily digested beans, popular in the Southern United States and in African countries, marinate well in salads and combine well with rice as in the popular southern dish, Hoppin' John. Black-eyed peas require no presoaking due to their thin skins, and even fall apart if ovecooked.

Black Soybeans: More easily digested and richer tasting than their blond counterparts, black soybeans have a nutrient value similar to the other soys. Presoaking black soybeans is essential for proper cooking, which takes anywhere from two to three hours. When the beans are tender, simply sprinkle with shoyu and chopped green onions, and stir in a spoonful of mustard for a delicious but uncomplicated bean dish.

Chickpeas (Garbanzos, Cecis): These round, light tan beans seem to please even people who feel luke-warm about most other beans. Perhaps it is their subtle, almost nutty flavor which makes them popular in salads or as the primary ingredient in purées such as hummus. Chickpeas characteristically retain their shape as well as their firmness even when fully cooked and tender, making them attractive additions to salads or vegetable stews.

Great Northern: The creamy texture and simple flavor of Great Northerns make them great thickeners in sauces or soups as well as a basis of herb dips and spreads. When kept whole, Great Northerns often appear in baked bean dishes — Italian favorites like pasta e fagioli, or in cassoulet-type preparations.

Kidney: Probably the most familiar bean in the United States, burgundy red kidneys are featured in the New Orleans favorite red beans and rice, and in many chili variations. If cooked gently, they retain their kidney-like shape, and are ideal for use in a marinated bean or pasta salad. Since kidney beans hold their own in the company of strong seasonings, their flavor is enhanced by onion, garlic, oregano, and cumin, or, for the heat-loving eater, cayenne and hot jalalpeño peppers.

Lentils: Cultivated for 9,000 to 10,000 years, longer than any other legume, lentils figure significantly in the traditional cuisine of many European, Asian, and African cultures. These tiny, flat, round beans can cook without presoaking in 20 to 30 minutes, making them the quickest beans to prepare. When combined with a bay leaf, *kombu*, chopped onions, garlic, and carrots, lentils make a deeply-flavored soup. With other seasonings, lentils can become rich pâtés or lemony marinated salads.

Red Lentils: Smaller and more rapidly cooked than their brown or green cousins, red lentils are milder tasting beans which are paticularly popular in Indian dishes. Although coral-colored while raw and dry, the red lentil turns creamy yellow when fully cooked.

Lima Beans (Fordhooks, Butter Beans): Commonly found both dry and fresh as well as in small and large varieties, limas have a mild taste adaptable to almost any preparation. They can be cooked until creamy textured and blended in soups or sauces.

Navy Beans: Navy beans look like a small variety of Great Northern beans. Because they hold their shape when gently cooked, they can be used with pasta in minestrone soup and in baked bean recipes, as well as in salads tossed with greens and a vinaigrette.

Pinto Beans: Slightly smaller than kidney beans and speckled with brown (when raw), pintos are often used interchangeably with kidneys in many popular southwestern and Mexican dishes. When cooked, pinto beans turn a pale pink and have a creamy interior texture. Wonderful when seasoned with garlic, cumin, peppers, cilantro, and/or oregano, the mellow flavored pinto is at home in combinations with corn, rice, tortillas, or salads.

Soybeans: The earliest recorded use of these round, pale ivory beans dates back almost 4,000 years in China. So crucial was the soybean to survival in the ancient Orient that it was regarded as one of the "Two Sacred Grains," and commonly was referred to as "the magic bean." Soybeans have the most complete protein available in the vegetable kingdom, and in fact are the nutritional king of the legumes. An easily absorbed iron occurs in the hulls of soybeans, and other valuable nutrients — such as calcium, some essential B vitamins, vitamin E, and polyunsaturated oils (about 20 percent of its total contents) — are available in both the prepared whole beans and in soy products. Although the U. S. produces two-thirds of the world's supply of soybeans, only 2 percent of soybeans grown here are actually used for human consumption.

Soy foods have been shown in a number of studies to help reduce heart damaging tri-glycerides, regulate the intestines, enhance estrogen function, and potentially guard against gallstone formation.

One drawback of soybeans is their long cooking time. There are several recipes from soy-derived foods, like tempeh (whole cooked and fermented soy beans) and tofu. Tempeh, is more easily digested than simple soybeans because the fermentation process used in its production breaks down their troublesome oligosaccharides. Tempeh can support strong flavors and makes rich pâtés, seasoned stews, or, if accompanied by mustard and sauerkraut, hearty sandwiches. For the smoothest flavor, use tempeh when it is fresh and not totally riddled with dark veining. Tofu is prepared from soy milk, has a higher protein and fat content than most legumes — although totally free of cholesterol — and is easily digested even by most newcomers to legume foods. Available in a range of forms labelled as extra-firm to soft, tofu can best be described as having a custard-like to soft cheesy texture and a bland, unimposing taste which easily absorbs accompanying flavors. Tofu can be cooked quickly in a variety of pleasing dishes from marinated and grilled kebabs to pasta sauces and creamy dips.

Split Peas: Like lentils, split peas are easily digested and require relatively little cooking time without presoaking. In fact, split peas cook within 30 to 40 minutes, making a smooth, full-bodied soup which can be simply but perfectly flavored — for example, with chopped onion, carrot, bay leaf, kombu, and miso or shoyu. Crisp croutons seasoned with herbs or garlic make an ideal complement to the "creamy" texture and flavor of split pea soup, but there are many possible variations, reflecting seasonal adjustments as well as personal preference. Although green split peas are the most familiar variety in the U. S., yellow split peas are classically used in peas porridge and in Scandanavian stews.

MISO

Phillip Shubik, in the *Potential Carcinogenicity of Food Additives and Contaminants,* stated, "Since it may not be possible to remove all carcinogenic materials from the environment, methods to mitigate or neutralize their harmful effects should be sought." Surprisingly, the sought-after substance may not emerge from chemical labs and test tube concoctions but from less obvious sources: fermented soybeans and sea vegetables. Miso (pronounced mee-so), a deep and rich-tasting fermented soybean purée, appears frequently in this book as a recipe ingredient, especially in soups and condiments. A generous provider of calcium and trace minerals, an enhancer of protein, and a supplier of other nutrients, miso boasts properties that work almost like magic in the body. The most remarkable asset of miso is its capacity to ward off the fearsome consequences of irradiation, and to protect against damage from heavy metals and other pollutants which can accumulate in body tissue. When the atomic bomb was dropped on Nagasaki in 1945, Dr. Tatsuichiro Akizuki, a director of Urakame Hospital in the city, made certain that his entire staff was fed miso soup daily. Radiation exposure was unavoidable; his hospital was located only one mile from the center of the blast. In follow-up studies, the doctor discovered that none of his co-workers suffered from the devastating effects of atomic radiation. Other comparable groups were not as fortunate. In his book *Nagasaki, 1945* (Quartet Books, 1981), he hypothesized that a component of miso might have been the protective factor.

Almost 30 years later in 1972, as reported by Shurtleff and Aoyagi in *The Book of Miso* (Ballantine Books, 1976), Japanese scientists who were intrigued by Dr. Akizuki's records, identified zybilocin (dipicolinic acid) in miso. This substance, a by-product of the natto and miso yeasts, has been found to bind with heavy metals and radioactive particles to form inert salts, which are either eliminated from the body or stored in a harmless form.

Miso has other benefits. It is richly endowed with lecithin and linoleic acid. Each of these minerals dissolves, and then eliminates damaging cholesterol and fat accumulations. Another benefit: An acid blood condition is like a door thrust open to disease; but according to trational oriental medicine, miso helps to shut this door by modulating an acid blood level into a healthy alkaline level. An additional bonus: present in all non-pasteurized misos are active enzymes, particularly lactobacillus, which breed beneficial flora and aid the digestive process, increasing total nutrient absorption.

CAUTION ABOUT SODIUM CONTAINING FOODS:

Please don't assume because miso has been shown to be beneficial to the system, that "if some is good, then more must be better." The sodium content of most misos ranges between 11 and 13 percent. It's best to keep this in mind when stirring miso into your soups and sauces. (A general guideline in preparing soups is to use anywhere from 1/2 to 1 teaspoon of miso purée per cup of soup.) Nothing you prepare should ever taste "salty." In fact, initially, your foods should seem like they could use another sprinkling of salt. Very quickly your taste buds will become sensitized to sodium, and a generous pinch of sea salt in a pot of rice, a spoonful of miso in a kettle of soup, or a dash of shoyu (traditionally fermented varieties) will enliven the flavor. In contrast, oversalting foods will dull the taste buds, diminishing sensitivity to the natural flavors of foods. Of course, once foods with a significant inherent sodium content, such as red meats and hard cheeses, are no longer part of your diet, the judicious use of miso and shoyu can be incorporated to enhance your eating.

Contrary to prevailing opinion, salt may not pose a grave health risk *if used in moderation.* Although some people are "salt sensitive," that is, they are unable to excrete salt and thus retain water which can elevate blood pressure as well as disrupt important chemical balances, current information suggests that not everyone need become nervous about salt consumption. This does not mean unrestrained use of salt or salty condiments, but the sparing use in food preparation.

SEA VEGETABLES

If someone mentions treasures from the sea, we usually picture pirate chests bursting with gold pieces. Actually, simple plants growing in the ocean yield rich bounties for our health and well-being — a *real* treasure.

Put aside your vitamin capsules and mineral supplements. Sea grown vegetables, unfamiliar to most Americans, but more customary to natives of coastal locales in Scandinavia, Scotland, Ireland, and Asia, furnish copious amounts of vitamins A, B, and C. One variety of sea vegetable, *kombu,* which frequently appears in this book as a soup ingredient or part of a bean preparation, has three times more B vitamins than milk or milk products. Ergosterol, which converts to vitamin D in the body, is richly supplied by all sea vegetables.

Sea vegetables are also high in minerals. For example, an average portion of hiziki provides 14 times the quantity of calcium found in a comparable serving of milk. *Dulse,* a red sea vegetable still commonly eaten in Scotland and Nova Scotia, and up until the 1930s, a best-seller in certain seaboard locations even in this country, can claim one of the highest concentrations of iron found in any food.

Besides this rich inventory of vitamins, minerals, and basic nutrients, sea vegetables are endowed with potent healing properties. Research has found that cancer patients excrete vital amounts of zinc. Kelp readily replenishes this essential element, which is crucial to both antibody and cell-mediated immune functions. In the mid 1960s, an astonishing medical discovery showed that sodium alginates, compounds which occur naturally in kelp and other sea vegetables, actually inhibit the absorption of radioactive strontium and cadmium. In research at the Gastro-Intestinal Research Laboratory at McGill University in Montreal in 1964 and 1968, alginates demonstrated the ability to bind with heavy, toxic molecules within the intestines to form insoluble salts, which are excreted from the body. In addition, inherent in brown sea vegetables of the *Laminaria* group are potent anti-cancer compounds, which as shown by Yamamoto and Takahashi in *Japan Journal of Experimental Medicine* (1974) not only help protect against cancer, but appear to inhibit or suppress already existing tumors. Add to these benefits an additional bonus: when fed a diet containing sea vegetables, animals on a high-fat program in a number of studies showed a significant reduction of plasma cholesterol levels unlike the control group.

A NOTE ABOUT EXOTICA

Certain exotic or less familiar food items, like shiitake mushrooms, burdock, and daikon, have often been selected as ingredients in many instances because of specific, documented health benefits as well as taste and texture. Take grated daikon radish, for example. This long white radish root, traditionally accompanying tempura and broiled fish in Japanese meals, contains not only diastaste, a digestive enzyme, but an organic substance which controls lipid peroxide, a significant factor in liver and artery disorders. (Lipid peroxide forms by oxidation when fats in foods are heated.) An interesting study at Tokushima University reported in the *Mainich Daily News,* January 15, 1988, showed levels of lipid peroxide in fried foods which were smothered in grated daikon fell dramatically — to one seventh of the total fat content measured immediately after frying. Identical foods which had not been covered with grated daikon maintained high lipid peroxide counts.

Another unusual vegetable item is burdock root, Arctium lappa, a member of the dandelion family. Not only does this earthy root vegetable have a pleasing taste and aroma when sautéed with carrots and other familiar vegetables and is nutrient rich, burdock also contains some very special, potentially healing properties. It has been reported to contain benzaldehyde, a compound which has shown positive activity against inoperable carcinoma tumors. ("Antitumor Activity of Benzaldehyde", *Cancer Treatments Reports,* 1980.)

Shiitake mushrooms figure prominently in the traditional cuisines of China and Japan, and in recent years have become a popular gourmet item in the U.S. This mushroom, *Lentinus edodes,* is used medicinally in Japan to stimulate disease resistance, and in the last two to three decades has gained support from scientific research. For instance, shiitakes contain specific polysaccharides which augment the effectiveness of the immune system. One in particular, lentinan, has demonstrated the capacity to produce dramatic regression of sarcoma tumors without toxicity, as reported in *Cancer Research,* 1970.

MORE THAN THE SUM OF ITS PARTS

There is a lot of reliable information to help us determine what we should eat. But it would be futile to prescribe a diet with only sound nutritional principles to recommend it. Intellectual appeal is not compelling enough to hold us permanently to any dietary plan we don't truly enjoy. If we feel forced to swallow our meals, while pinching our noses as if taking nasty medicine, the likelihood of staying with a healthy regimen is negligible.

Food is much more than the sum of its nutrients; more even than the total synergy of chemical components. Food is convivial social gatherings, an expression and satisfaction of our deepest personal needs, our connection to the earth, our first and most fundamental link to other human beings.

When an infant wails because of nagging hunger in his or her belly, and then is picked up tenderly and nursed or fed, the easing of this hunger and discomfort with food is translated gradually into larger feelings — of love, human warmth, and connectedness. From then on, the provision of food can be equated with caring. Food is warm, chewy cookies which relieve the tensions of the school day; immense portions of steaming, fresh pasta which accompany travel tales of long-missed friends; a cool fruit confection which takes the sting out of a burning insult. To deny these non-nutritional ways in which food nourishes and sustains us is to ignore factors essential to making a successful switch from one eating style to another — regardless of how obviously sensible the new dietary regimen is.

COMPOSING A MEAL

Once determined to overhaul my dietary habits, I discovered it was not as difficult to discard long-held myths about the necessity of milk as it was to scrap former notions about what constituted a meal. Dinner had always seemed synonymous with some protein entrée and anything else served on the plate was deemed of little consequence. Even before learning the alphabet, I had learned to ask, "What's for dinner?" — which really meant, "Are we having chicken or beef tonight, and if chicken, will it be fried or broiled?" Any accompaniments to the dinner, such as potatoes, white rice, a white-flour pasta, some frozen vegetable, and a salad, were in my eyes just peripheral items. Granted, what I was accustomed to eating was relatively clean and simple, better than much of the fatty, chemicalized, processed entrées available today, but it still focused too much on animal protein without appropriate emphasis on grains and greens.

Now I understand that meals are a composite. For example, when planning dinner, my first consideration is which grain and what style of preparation to use, given the weather (damp and chilly vs. warm and humid), and companion dishes. Then I select a bean dish or other concentrated protein which will complement the grain item and be complemented by a soup, green vegetable, possibly a sea vegetable preparation (either incorporated in another dish or served as a separate side dish), and usually a sweet or orange-colored vegetable. Obviously, there are variations on this type of arrangement, and I certainly need not make fresh preparations from scratch each day. If there is buttercup squash left over from the previous night's dinner, a squash purée soup could start the meal. If there happens to be sufficient millet left in the refrigerator and if I have prepared a double portion of chickpeas, I could easily serve millet-chickpea patties. And if some cooked hiziki or arame are also available, these sea vegetables can also be mixed into the patties. (You will note that I try to avoid the texture monotony and color redundancy which could occur had a puréed red lentil dish followed the creamed squash soup for instance.) By using leftover portions and by deliberately preparing excess quantities, I can compose a fresh and complete meal without investing a great deal of time.

When planning a meal, it is important to consider visual appeal, a pleasing combination of textures and colors, and the inclusion of the full complement of flavors — sweet, salty, sour, bitter, and pungent. Adding a garnish of parsley or chopped green onions, or arranging food attractively by juxtaposing bright, gently cooked, slightly crisp greens alongside a smooth orange squash purée, are not superfluous efforts. Any meal should satisfy all senses and be uplifting. There are so many subtle, nonmeasurable ways in which food nourishes us beyond simply eating to refuel. Even from a purely biochemical standpoint, a number of studies indicates that people who take continual pleasure in eating actually absorb a higher percentage of the nutrient value in their food. Of course, if you were feeling famished and someone shoved a full dinner plate in front of you covered with a large mound of rice, a pile of plain beans and a few strips of overcooked greens, it might satisfy your hunger and even your nutritional requirements, but in some subtle yet significant way, this meal would starve you. For this reason, spend an extra 60 seconds and think of your meal's presentation — it's a good investment.

One final word of caution: disappointment is inevitable when we try to create a substitute for a cherished food or special treat which we once loved but have decided to forego. There is no way to duplicate certain flavors and textures, and our anticipation and expectations when hearing words like "pizza" will be frustrated if a beet sauce is substituted for tomato, and if instead of cheese a grated grain which seems to melt is used. Simulated or mock tastes cannot possibly match the standards of comparison in our memory banks. For example, cheese is cheese. Grated mochi, despite the current hype in certain circles, will not produce a truly cheesey texture or taste. Instead, what usually happens is that we discover new favorites to delight our senses. A few weeks ago, just out of curiosity, my husband Keith and I sampled a cannoli at a very fine Italian restaurant in Washington, D. C. Neither of us could swallow the small mouthfuls on our forks. It was so overwhelming and cloyingly sweet that it almost hurt. Politeness prevented us from spitting it out and saying, "Yuck!" Had we attempted at home to create a mock ricotta filling, chances are that we would have been dissatisfied. But a homemade almond cream-filled profiterolle, gently sweetened with rice syrup and generously topped with a fresh strawberry sauce or carob glaze, is a superb treat which will not leave us feeling ill, and even on the most festive occasions will produce as many "oohs" and "ahs" as a comparable sugary one.

EFFICIENCY STRATEGIES

It's easy to feel overwhelmed when first transforming meals into a natural foods affair. "I could be in the kitchen all day preparing meals!" is the lament heard most frequently when people first start cooking whole grains, beans, and accompanying dishes. Even kitchen veterans can feel like novices with what seems to be labor-intensive preparations and a long list of exotic-sounding ingredients. How to provide healthy, tasteful meals, given real time constraints, represents a daily dilemma. While wanting to be conscientious about what we eat, work and other commitments propel us towards the quick and easy. Thankfully, there are some simple strategies which can minimize "starting-from-scratch" kitchen time without compromising the wholesomeness of your food. For example, in one hour, you can prepare the basis for several days' meals.

- Put some beans in a pot with a piece of kombu and water. Cover and simmer.
- Place rinsed rice or any whole grain of your choice in another pot. Add a pinch of sea salt and 2 times the amount of water. Cover and simmer.
- Place vegetable pieces or cuttings such as carrots chunks, onion slices or wedges, parsley, and others in a soup pot. Add 4 quarts of water, a generous pinch of sea salt, and simmer covered.

Happily, these pots can simmer independent of your attention while you focus on other business or perhaps read the Sunday newspaper. Once prepared, these foods can be stored in large glass or plastic containers in the refrigerator. (Or cooked beans and grains can be packed for freezer storage in individual serving portions.) How do you translate these unadorned beans and grains and soup base into an appealing meal? The following represents just a sampling of possibilities.

• Cooked beans can be used with boiled elbow macaroni noodles, chopped green onions, radishes, and celery in a salad; puréed and seasoned to fill pita pockets; added to soup stock; made into a stew with vegetables; or possibly mixed with a mustardy sauce in a burrito.

• Grains can be used in a salad tossed with chopped fresh vegetables and a vinaigrette dressing; stewed with vegetables; stir-fried; seasoned with grated onion and sea salt and cooked in a lightly oiled skillet as a pattie; added to a soup; combined with vegetables, seasoned bread crumbs, toasted seeds, and baked as a casserole; or simply steamed with mushroom gravy.

• The basic vegetable soup can be transformed into mushroom barley soup; puréed with beans for a creamy bean dish; served as a broth with noodles; or tofu and broccoli can be added for a one-dish meal.

Within weeks, you will most likely discover that getting a wholesome and appealing dinner on the table seems a little less complicated and time consuming. Like any endeavor, familiarity will bring ease.

COOKING EQUIPMENT
Avoid using aluminum cookware, as some evidence suggests that with heat, salty as well as acidic foods cause a leaching of aluminum into the foods themselves. Aluminum can be toxic. It has a possible association with several disorders, not the least of which is Alzheimer's. Although it is uncertain whether the presence of aluminum in brain tissue of Alzheimer patients precedes or follows as a consequence of the disorder, why risk the unnecessary? Instead, stainless steel, cast iron (which does enhance iron intake, a necessary trace mineral), ceramic ware, glass or pyrex, and porcelin are recommended options for cooking equipment.

A stainless steel pressure cooker can be an ally in preparing a number of beans and grains. Pressure-cooked rice, as an example, requires less water than boiled, resulting in a fuller, less diluted flavor.

It is my hope that this book will enable you to feed your bodies in a healthy way, and also your hearts with pleasure, variety, and delight. Bon Appetit!

WORKS CITED

"Diet and Cell Growth Modulation by Ammonia," Visek, W. J.; *The American Journal of Clinical Nutrition;* October, 1978.

Diet, Lifestyle, and Mortality in China: A Study of the Characteristics of 65 Countries; J. Chen, T. Colin Campbell, Li Junyao, and Richard Peto; Oxford University Press, Cornell University Press, and the People's Publishing House, Bejing, 1991.

Dr. Dean Ornish's Program for Reversing Heart Disease; Ornish, Dean; Random House; October, 1991.

"Food Contaminants: Animal Growth Promoters (Antibiotic Residues);" *Handbook of Naturally Occuring Food Toxicants;* Siddiquw, I.H.; Rechigal, M. Jr., Ed.; CRC Press, 1983.

GLOSSARY OF INGREDIENTS AND FOOD ITEMS

AGAR: A natural, flavorless, colorless, odorless gelling ingredient, available in bars and flakes, produced from sea vegetables.

AGE: Deep-fried tofu.

AMASAKE: A pudding-like dessert or sweetener produced by fermenting sweet rice with koji bacteria.

ARAME: A calcium-rich sea vegetable which gives a subtle sweetness to salads, soups, and side-dishes.

ARROWROOT: A thickening agent processed from the starch of a tropical tuber.

BANCHA TWIG TEA: A non-aromatic hot or cold beverage, also called kukicha, made from the roasted twigs of the bancha bush.

BARLEY MALT: A concentrated sweetener produced with sprouted barley which is cooked into a thick syrup.

BIFUN: Delicate, quick-cooking noodles made from rice flour.

BONITO FLAKES: Dried, smoked flakes of fish, shaved from the Bonito fish (a type of tuna).

BURDOCK: A hardy, long brown root vegetable valued for its mineral content and energy-boosting effects.

CILANTRO: The fresh, aromatic leaves of the coriander plant (also known as Chinese parsley).

DAIKON: A long, white radish root which aids in digesting fatty foods and in the elimination of excess fluids.

FU: Steamed and dried sheets or cakes of wheat gluten; a valuable protein source.

GOMASIO: A condiment made with dry roasted sesame seeds ground with sea salt.

JINENJO: A Japanese wild mountain yam which is starchy, but not sweet.

JINENJO SOBA: A noodle combining jinenjo with buckwheat and whole wheat flours.

KANPYO: Strips of dried, edible gourd used as a garnish, for example, to tie vegetable bundles.

KANTEN: A gelatin using agar, which is cooked and dissolved in a sweetened liquid.

KINAKO (soy flour): A powder made from roasted, pulverized soybeans.

KOJI: Rice kernels injected with fermenting bacteria, used in the fermenting process to produce rice vinegar, sake, and amasake.

KOMBU: A dark green sea vegetable from the kelp family, used to enhance the flavor of soups, the nurient value and the digestibility of beans, and as a condiment.

KUZU (kudzu): A thickening agent made from the starch of the dried, powdered root.

MIRIN: Sweet rice wine primarily used for cooking; comparable to sherry.

MOCHI: Cooked sweetened rice which is seasoned and pounded to form dumplings or savory squares.

NORI: Thin sheets of crisp, pressed sea vegetables, especially high in vitamin A; said to reduce cholesterol and aid digestion of oily foods. When toasted lightly, nori can be used as a garnish, a condiment, or to wrap rice rolls.

RICE SYRUP: A mild sweetener made from malted brown rice and barley malt (maltose).

SEA SALT: Salt crystalized from ocean waters, generally free of additives, somewhat higher in trace minerals, and slightly lower in actual sodium chloride than land derived salts.

SEITAN (wheat meat): The gluten or protein portion of wheat, simmered in a seasoned broth and used like meat cutlets or in stews and sandwiches.

SHIITAKE: An oriental mushroom with documented health benefits; available fresh and dried.

SHOYU: A liquid seasoning which is the product of fermented and aged soybeans, wheat, sea salt, and water, and which is rich in digestive enzymes.

SOBA: A Japanese-style noodle made primarily or totally from buckwheat.

TAHINI: A rich paste made from ground sesame seeds used in dressings, dips, and sauces.

TAMARI: A naturally fermented liquid seasoning, similar to shoyu but without wheat.

TEMPEH: Tender cooked and fermented split soybeans, a rich source of high-quality protein.

TOFU: A soy product made from cooked soy milk.

UDON: A Japanese pasta made either totally from whole wheat or in combination with unbleached, sifted wheat.

UMEBOSHI: Tart, pickled Japanese plums (loquats) generally used as condiments, and believed to aid indigestion and help alkalize the digestive process.

UMEBOSHI "VINEGAR" (umesu): The liquid from the pickling process of umeboshi plums, used like a vinegar, but is non-acidic.

WAKAME: Delicate in flavor and texture, this green leafy sea vegetable is quite high in thiamin, niacin, and vitamin C as well as calcium and other minerals, and makes a perfect ingredient for soup and fresh salads.

WASABE: A Japanese horseradish sold usually in powdered, packaged form.

BUYING SOURCES

A number of ingredients used in these recipes may not be available in your local grocery store. Yet, super markets are now introducing many of the items which, until recently, might have been difficult to locate, such as, tofu, shiitake mushrooms (dried and fresh), rice vinegar, dried beans, brown rice, even toasted sesame oil and organic fruit juices. A few items like age pouches can be found in Japanese or Chinese groceries in metropolitan areas. However, natural food stores still remain the most likely source for the majority of ingredients that you will need in preparing these recipes.

If you are unable to locate recipe ingredients, you can write or call one of the following mail order companies (listed alphabetically) for their natural foods catalogues.

Gold Mine Natural Food Company
1947 30th Street
San Diego, CA 92102
1-800-475-FOOD

Mountain Ark Trading Company
120 South East Avenue
Fayeteville, AR 72701
01-800-643-8909

Natural Lifestyle Supplies
16 Lookout Drive
Asheville, N.C. 28804
1-800-752-2775

RECIPES

All recipes in this cookbook make approximately six to eight servings.

APPETIZERS

Tempeh Dip or Dressing

8 ounces tempeh, steamed or simmered
½ cup water
2 tablespoons lemon juice
1 tablespoon olive OR canola oil
1 clove garlic, minced
½ teaspoon sea salt

Blend all ingredients in a food processor or blender to make a dip for crackers or cut fresh vegetables. A tablespoon or more of water can be added to thin dip to desired consistency.

Tofu "Cheese"

1 16-ounce package firm tofu
  miso to cover
1 teaspoon ginger juice (optional)
¼ teaspoon sesame oil (optional)

Parboil the tofu in water with a pinch of sea salt for a few minutes. Drain and rinse with cold water; drain again. Cut into ½-inch thick slices and place on slanted cutting board covered with a cotton towel. Press covered tofu by putting another cutting board or a bamboo mat topped with a weight for 15 minutes; remove. Spread miso on all sides of pressed tofu slices with a knife; wrap in cheesecloth. Place in uncovered glass or ceramic bowl and allow to stand for 2 to 3 days out of direct light. Wipe miso from tofu with the side of a knife or with a clean towel; mash or purée with ginger juice and sesame oil, if desired. Use as a spread for rice cakes or crackers.

Hummus

2   cups cooked chickpeas
3 - 4 tablespoons lemon juice
2   cloves garlic, minced
2   tablespoons tahini (optional)
2   tablespoons olive oil (optional)
1   teaspoon sea salt
1   teaspoon cumin

Purée all ingredients in a blender or food processor. A few drops of water can be added to thin dip to desired consistency. Serve with warm whole wheat pita bread rounds cut into wedges.

Guacamole

1   large ripe avocado
1   teaspoon fresh lemon juice
2   tablespoons grated fresh onion
¼   teaspoon sea salt, or to taste
¼   teaspoon chopped fresh cilantro (optional)
1   pinch cayenne pepper

Cut the avocado in half; discard pit. Scoop out the flesh; sprinkle with lemon juice and mash with a fork in medium bowl until smooth. Stir in salt, cilantro, if desired, and cayenne pepper. Serve as a dip with cut fresh vegetables or crackers. Or, spoon teaspoonfuls over fajitas, burritos, or other Mexican foods as a garnish.

Variation: Guacamole can be mixed with ½ cup silken tofu for a creamier consistency.

Note: Avocado is very high in natural oils and is not recommended for those following a low-fat diet.

Tempeh-Stuffed Mushrooms

12- 14 large mushrooms, cleaned
    Olive oil
1   medium onion, minced
1   clove garlic, crushed
¼   teaspoon sea salt, or to taste
¼   teaspoon dried basil
4   ounces tempeh, crumbled
3   tablespoons dry bread crumbs

Preheat oven to 375°F. Lightly oil 8 x 12-inch glass baking dish.

Remove mushroom stems; mince and set aside. Lightly coat the bottom of large skillet with olive oil; place over medium heat. Sauté onion, garlic, and sea salt for 3 to 4 minutes or until translucent. Add minced mushroom stems and basil; sauté 2 to 3 minutes. Add tempeh; mix well. Remove from heat. Spoon mixture evenly into mushroom caps. Place filled caps into prepared baking dish. Sprinkle bread crumbs over filling. Cover with foil and bake for 15 minutes or until caps are tender. Remove foil and bake 2 to 3 minutes.

Spring Rolls

    Canola oil
6 - 8 fresh shiitake mushrooms, sliced OR 6 dried shiitake
    mushrooms, soaked and drained according to package
    directions, sliced
2   cloves garlic, crushed
1½ cups shredded napa cabbage
1½ cups bean sprouts
3   green onions, chopped
1   teaspoon grated fresh ginger root
¼   teaspoon sea salt, or to taste
1   pinch white pepper
2   tablespoons kuzu, dissolved in 2 tablespoons water
6   spring roll wrappers, covered to keep moist

Lightly coat the bottom of a large skillet with oil; sauté garlic and mushrooms over medium heat. Cover; continue to cook over medium heat 2 to 3 minutes. Stir in cabbage, bean sprouts, onions, and ginger. Sprinkle with salt and pepper. Add dissolved kuzu mixture, stirring so no lumps form. Remove from heat.

To assemble Spring Rolls, place 2 rounded teaspoonfuls of vegetable mixture near one end of one wrapper. Fold nearest end over filling, then fold the sides over slightly. Roll over and moisten end with water to seal. Repeat with remaining vegetable mixture and wrappers. Keep finished rolls under a damp towel until ready to cook.

Pour approximately 4 cups oil into a large pot. Over high heat, heat oil until it registers 375°F on a candy thermometer. Using a slotted metal spoon, carefully place a few Spring Rolls in oil; fry 5 to 6 minutes or until golden, turning once. Remove cooked rolls; drain on paper towels. Repeat with remaining Spring Rolls. Spring Rolls can be kept warm in a how-heat oven until ready to serve.

Tofu Dip

8   ounces silken tofu, drained
2   cloves garlic, crushed
1   tablespoon grated fresh onion
1   tablespoon almond butter (optional)
1   teaspoon umeboshi paste OR 1 tablespoon fresh lemon
    juice and ½ teaspoon sea salt
¼   teaspoon dried basil
1   pinch black pepper

Purée all ingredients in a food processor or blender. A few drops of water can be added to thin dip to desired consistency. Serve with cut fresh vegetables or crackers.

Tapenade

24 pitted Mediterranean black olives
3   tablespoons fresh lemon juice
1½ tablespoons capers
1   tablespoon olive oil
1   clove garlic, crushed ·
1   teaspoon prepared yellow mustard

Purée all ingredients in a food processor or blender. Additional lemon juice and olive oil can be added to thin to desired consistency. Serve as a vegetable dip, canape, or pasta sauce. Refrigerate leftovers.

Note: Olives have a very high fat content and are not reccommended for those following an extremely low-fat diet.

SOUPS

Basic Vegetable Stock

1   gallon water
1   large onion, cut into 8 wedges
2   carrots, sliced
1   parsnip, sliced
2   stalks celery, sliced
2   leeks, thoroughly cleaned and sliced
1   cup chopped fresh parsley
¼   cup chopped fresh dill weed (optional)
2 - 3 cloves garlic, crushed
½   teaspoon dried thyme OR dried basil
     Sea salt to taste
     Black pepper to taste

Place all ingredients in a large soup pot; bring to a boil over high heat. Reduce heat and simmer 45 minutes to 1 hour. Strain into a large storage jar; discard vegetables. Cool to room temperature; cover and refrigerate for use in recipes calling for Basic Vegetable Stock.

Vegetable Soup

1   large onion, minced
     Olive or canola oil
5 - 6 shallots, peeled and minced OR 3 green onions, chopped
2   leeks, thoroughly cleaned and finely chopped
     Sea salt to taste
2 - 3 cloves garlic, crushed
1   parsnip, cut into matchsticks
1   large carrot, cut into matchsticks
1   large turnip, cut into matchsticks
6   cups Basic Vegetable Stock (recipe above) OR water
¼   teaspoon dried thyme
     Black pepper to taste
2 - 3 tablespoons miso, or to taste
4   tablespoons chopped fresh parsley

Lightly coat the bottom of soup pot with oil; place over high heat. Add onion, shallots, and leeks. Reduce heat to medium and sauté for 3 to 4 minutes, adding sea salt. Stir in garlic; cook, covered, for 2 minutes. Add remaining vegetables, stock, and seasonings; simmer 30 minutes or until vegetables are tender. Scoop out approximately ½ cup of soup; pour over miso and stir until dissolved. Stir miso mixture into soup. Bring soup back to a simmer; ladle into bowls. Garnish each serving with parsley

French Onion Soup with Herbed Croutons

3   large onions, halved and thinly sliced into half-moons
    Olive oil
1   pinch sea salt
1   pinch black pepper
6   cups Basic Vegetable Stock (recipe page 57) OR water
1   bay leaf
2   tablespoons shoyu
2   tablespoons miso
1   tablespoon dry white wine (optional)
    Chopped fresh parsley, for garnish
    Herbed Croutons (recipe follows), optional

Lightly coat the bottom of soup pot with oil; place over high heat. Add onions; sauté 2 to 3 minutes. Sprinkle with salt and pepper. Cover; reduce heat to low. Cook onions 5 minutes or until they appear to "sweat." Add vegetable stock and bay leaf. Bring just to a boil; reduce heat to low. Stir in shoyu; cover and simmer for 20 minutes, Add wine, if desired. Scoop out approximately ½ cup of soup; pour over miso and stir until dissolved. Stir miso mixture into soup. Return soup to a simmer (do not boil). Ladle into bowls. Garnish each serving with parsley and Herbed Croutons, if desired.

HERBED CROUTONS

    Olive oil
2   cloves garlic
1   tablespoon chopped fresh basil OR 1 teaspoon dried basil
¼   teaspoon dried thyme
1   pinch sea salt, or to taste
3   slices day-old bread, cut into 1-inch squares

continued following page

Lightly coat heated bottom of a large skillet with oil; place over high heat. Stir in garlic and/or herbs; sprinkle with sea salt, if desired. Toss bread cubes in skillet to coat. Set aside until ready to use. (If desired, Herbed Croutons can be made more crispy by placing them in a baking pan in a 300°F oven. Bake for 10 minutes.)

Miso Soup

6 cups water (including shiitake soaking water)
4 - 6 dried shiitake mushrooms
   Water
½ ounce fresh wakame (a 10- to 12-inch strip) OR ½ cup dried wakame, soaked and drained according to package directions
   Canola oil
1 large onion, halved and thinly sliced into half-moons
1-2 tablespoons shoyu
2 tablespoons miso, or to taste
1 - 2 green onions, thinly sliced, for garnish

Soak mushrooms in 1 cup of water for 10 minutes or until pliable; reserve soaking liquid. Remove knobby stems; discard. Slice caps; set aside. Add enough water to reserved soaking liquid to measure 6 cups. Remove tough center "stipe" from wakame and slice the fronds into thin strips. Add mushrooms and wakame to water mixture in a large soup pot over high heat.

Meanwhile, lightly brush heated bottom of skillet with oil; place over high heat. Sauté onions about 5 minutes or until translucent; add to soup mixture in pot. Bring to a boil; reduce heat to medium. Add shoyu; cover and simmer 15 to 20 minutes. Scoop out approximately ½ cup soup; pour over miso and stir until dissolved. Stir into soup and simmer over low heat, uncovered, 2 to 3 minutes. Ladle into bowls; garnish each serving with green onions.

Variation: Broccoli, noodles, tofu, carrots, Chinese cabbage, root vegetables, and/or fresh grated ginger root can be added to soup to vary and enhance flavor.

Sour and Hot Soup

6   dried shiitake mushrooms
½   cup water
    Basic Vegetable Stock (recipe page 60) OR water (about
    4½ cups)
2   cups shredded napa cabbage
¼   cup arame, soaked, rinsed, and drained (optional)
1   tablespoon shoyu
2   rounded tablespoons kuzu, dissolved in ¼ cup cold water
1   teaspoon grated fresh ginger root
⅛   teaspoon white pepper (optional)
4   ounces firm tofu, cut into ½-inch cubes (optional)
2   tablespoons brown rice vinegar
1   teaspoon sesame oil
1   tablespoon miso, or to taste
⅓   cup chopped green onions, for garnish

Cover mushrooms with water and soak for 15 minutes or until tender. Drain; reserve soaking water. Remove knobby stems; discard. Slice caps. Add enough vegetable stock to reserved soaking liquid to measure 5 cups; pour into large soup pot over high heat. Add napa, arame, and shoyu. Bring to a boil; reduce heat to low. Simmer, covered, for 5 minutes. Stir in dissolved kuzu, ginger, and pepper. Simmer until soup is translucent and thickened, stirring often to avoid clumping. Add sliced mushrooms and tofu, if desired. Stir in vinegar and sesame oil. Scoop out about ½ cup soup; pour over miso and stir until dissolved. Stir into soup; simmer over low heat 1 to 2 minutes. Ladle into bowls. Garnish each serving with chopped green onions.

Cabbage-Fennel Soup

1   large onion, sliced
    Olive oil
1   pinch sea salt, or to taste
½   medium cabbage, shredded
2   stalks celery, chopped
12 inches wakame, soaked, deribbed, and cut into thin
    strips
¼   teaspoon dried basil

continued following page

1   fennel bulb, trimmed, quartered, and sliced
3 - 4 cloves garlic, crushed
4 - 5 cups Basic Vegetable Stock (recipe page 60) OR water
1   tablespoon brown rice vinegar
1   tablespoon shoyu
1   tablespoon miso, or to taste
¼   cup chopped parsley, for garnish

Lightly coat heated bottom of soup pot with oil; place over high heat. Sauté onion 2 to 3 minutes. Sprinkle with salt; cover and cook over low heat 3 to 4 minutes until onion is soft. Stir in cabbage, celery, wakame, fennel, and garlic; sauté 5 minutes until cabbage is translucent and wilted. Stir in vegetable stock, vinegar, and shoyu. Simmer, covered, 20 minutes. Scoop out approximately ½ cup soup; pour over miso and stir until dissolved. Stir into soup; simmer 1 minute over low heat. Ladle into bowls; garnish each serving with chopped parsley.

Leek Soup in Chickpea Broth

4 - 5 cups chickpea liquid
2 - 3 leeks, thoroughly cleaned and thinly sliced
1 - 2 tablespoons miso
1   large carrot, cut into matchsticks and steamed until tender

Bring chickpea liquid to a boil in large soup pot over high heat. Add leeks; reduce heat to low and simmer 15 to 20 minutes or until tender. Scoop out about ½ cup soup; pour over miso and stir until dissolved. Stir into soup; simmer 2 to 3 minutes over low heat. Ladle into bowls; top each serving with carrots.

*Chickpea liquid is the leftover broth from cooking 1 cup dried chickpeas, 1 bay leaf, and ½ strip kombu in 5 cups water.

Wild Rice and Mushroom Soup

8 - 10 large mushrooms, sliced
   Olive or canola oil
1   pinch sea salt
1/8 teaspoon black pepper (optional)
½   cup wild rice, rinsed with cool water and drained
2   leeks, thoroughly cleaned and thinly sliced
1   stalk celery, finely chopped
1   teaspoon grated fresh ginger root
1-2 cloves garlic
4   cups Basic Vegetable Stock (recipe page 60)
½   teaspoon dried thyme (optional)
1 - 2 tablespoons miso
2   tablespoons dry white wine
3   tablespoons chopped fresh parsley

Lightly coat the bottom of soup pot with oil; place over high heat. Sauté mushrooms and garlic with salt until liquid forms. Cover; continue cooking over low heat for 2 to 3 minutes. Stir in rice, leeks, celery, ginger, and vegetable stock. Simmer, uncovered, 35 minutes of until rice is tender. Scoop out about ½ cup soup; pour over miso and stir until dissolved. Stir into soup; simmer 2 minutes. Ladle into bowls; garnish each serving with parsley.

Mushroom-Barley Soup

6   dried shiitake mushrooms or 6-8 fresh white mushrooms
     Water
     Canola or olive oil
1   large onion, finely chopped
2/3 cup pearled barley
1   stalk celery, finely chopped
1   teaspoon sea salt, or to taste
1   tablespoon shoyu
1   bay leaf
½   teaspoon basil (optional)
1 - 2 tablespoons miso
3   tablespoons chopped fresh parsley

Soak mushrooms in enough water to cover until tender. Drain mushrooms; reserve soaking liquid. Remove and discard Knobby stems; slice caps.

continued following page

Lightly brush the bottom of soup pot with oil; place over high heat. Sauté onion 3 to 4 minutes or until translucent.

Meanwhile, add enough water to reserved soaking liquid to measure 6 cups. Add to onions with sliced mushrooms, barley, celery, salt, shoyu, bay leaf, and basil. Cover; bring to a boil. Reduce heat to low; simmer 20 minutes. Scoop out about ½ cup soup; pour over miso and stir until dissolved. Stir into soup; simmer 2 to 3 minutes. Ladle into bowls; garnish each serving with parsley.

Gingery Millet Soup

²/₃ cup millet
6   cups Basic Vegetable Stock (recipe page 60)
    Olive or canola oil
1   large onion, finely chopped
1   pinch sea salt
1   stalk celery, chopped
1   large carrot, sliced
¾   cup chopped fresh parsley
¼   teaspoon dried thyme
2 - 3 teaspoons grated fresh ginger root
1 - 2 tablespoons miso, or to taste

Rinse millet with cool water; drain. Toast millet in a large dry skillet over medium heat until fragrant, stirring occasionally. Add 2½ cups vegetable stock and simmer, covered, 30 minutes.

Meanwhile, lightly coat the bottom of soup pot with oil; place over high heat. Sauté onion 2 to 3 minutes or until slightly translucent. Sprinkle with salt; cover and cook over low heat 5 minutes. Stir in celery and carrot. Add remaining vegetable stock, cooked millet, parsley, thyme, and ginger. Simmer over low heat 3 minutes. Scoop out about ½ cup soup; pour over miso and stir until dissolved. Stir into soup; simmer 2 to 3 minutes. Ladle into bowls.

Creamy Mushroom Soup

       Olive oil
1   pound mushrooms, sliced
       Sea salt, to taste
       pinch of black pepper
1½   tablespoons sake (optional)
1   large onion, chopped
3 - 4 cloves garlic, minced
4½ cups Basic Vegetable Stock (recipe page 60) OR water
2/3   cup old-fashioned rolled oats (not instant)
1 - 2 tablespoons miso
¼   cup chopped fresh parsley

Lightly coat heated bottom of soup pot with oil; place over high heat. Sauté mushrooms with 1 pinch of salt 2 to 3 minutes or until liquid forms. Cover; reduce heat to low and cook 4 to 5 minutes or until tender. Stir in ½ tablespoon sake; simmer 1 minute. Remove mushroom mixture from pot; reserve. Recoat pot bottom with oil. Sauté onion with 1 pinch salt and garlic. Cover; cook over low heat 4 to 5 minutes or until onion is translucent. Stir in vegetable stock and oats. Cover; simmer 10 minutes. Purée soup with miso and remaining sake in batches in blender or food processor; return to pot. Stir in reserved mushroom mixture; simmer over low heat 3 minutes. Ladle into bowls; garnish each serving with parsley.

Note: Recipe can be prepared ahead of time and refrigerated. Reheat over low heat. Do not boil.

Squash Potage

1   large onion, chopped
       Canola oil
1   pinch sea salt
1   buttercup squash, baked, peeled, and seeded
3 - 4 cups water
¼   teaspoon EACH dried rosemary, thyme, and basil
1 - 2 tablespoons miso
¼   cup chopped fresh parsley

Lightly coat the bottom of soup pot with oil; place over high heat. Sauté

continued following page

onion 3 to 4 minutes or until translucent. Sprinkle with sea salt; cover and reduce heat to low. Cook 6 minutes; uncover and add water. Simmer 5 minutes. Purée squash in blender or food processor with onion mixture until smooth. Stir into pot. Stir in spices. Scoop out about ½ cup soup; pour over miso and stir until dissolved. Stir into pot; simmer over low heat 5 minutes. Ladle into bowls. Garnish each serving with parsley.

Corn Chowder

1   large onion, chopped
    Canola oil
1   pinch sea salt, or to taste
4   cups Basic Vegetable Stock (recipe page 60) OR water
3   large ears super-sweet corn, kernels removed and cobs
    reserved
2/3 cup old-fashioned rolled oats (not instant)
1   stalk celery, chopped
1 - 2 tablespoons miso

Lightly coat the bottom of soup pot with oil; place over high heat. Sauté onion 3 to 4 minutes or until translucent. Sprinkle with salt; cover and reduce heat to low. Cook 5 minutes; uncover and add vegetable stock, reserved corn cobs, and oats. Simmer 5 minutes; remove and discard cobs. Purée onion mixture in small batches in blender or food processor; return to pot. Stir in kernels and celery; cover and simmer 7 minutes or until corn is cooked and soup has thickened. Scoop out about ½ cup soup; pour over miso and stir until dissolved. Stir into soup; simmer over low heat 2 to 3 minutes. Ladle into bowls.

Lentil Soup

1   large onion, chopped
    Olive oil
2   stalks celery, diced
1   large carrot, cut into matchsticks
1   cup dry lentils, rinsed
6   cups water
1   clove garlic, crushed
1   bay leaf

¼   teaspoon *EACH* dried rosemary and basil
½   strip kombu
1   pinch sea salt
1   tablespoon miso
¼   cup chopped fresh parsley

Place all ingredients except salt, miso, and parsley in covered pressure cooker. Bring to pressure over high heat; reduce heat to low and cook for 20 minutes. Stir in salt. Scoop out about ½ cup soup; pour over miso and stir until dissolved. Stir into soup. Simmer 5 minutes over low heat; ladle into bowls. Garnish each serving with parsley.

Lentil-Noodle Soup

8   cups water
1   cup dry lentils, rinsed
    Olive oil
1   large onion, finely chopped
2 - 3 cloves garlic, crushed
1   pinch sea salt
½   cup dry pasta (such as somen or vermicelli), broken into
    1-inch pieces
½   cup chopped fresh cilantro
1   pinch red pepper flakes
1   tablespoon miso
2   tablespoons chopped green onion

In large soup pot, bring water and lentils to a rolling boil; reduce heat to low and simmer, covered, 30 minutes or until lentils are tender.

Meanwhile, lightly coat the bottom of large skillet with oil; place over high heat. Sauté onion and garlic with salt 3 to 4 minutes or until translucent. Stir in pasta and cilantro; reduce heat to low. Cover and cook 3 to 4 minutes. Stir mixture into soup pot; simmer 25 to 30 minutes.

Scoop out about ½ cup soup; pour over miso and stir until dissolved. Stir into soup; simmer over low heat 3 to 4 minutes. Ladle into bowls; garnish each serving with green onion.

Minestrone

1   cup dried kidney or pinto beans, rinsed and soaked OR 1
    16-ounce can beans, rinsed and drained
5   cups water
4   strips kombu
1   bay leaf
    Olive oil
1   large onion, chopped
2   cloves garlic, crushed
1   pinch sea salt, or to taste
1/8 teaspoon black pepper (optional)
2   cups Basic Vegetable Stock (recipe page 60) OR water
3   tablespoons chopped fresh parsley
1   8-ounce can chopped plum tomatoes (optional)
2   stalks celery, chopped
1   medium zucchini, sliced
1   large carrot, cut into matchsticks
1/2 teaspoon dried oregano
1/4 teaspoon dried basil
4   ounces dry elbow macaroni, cooked according to package
    directions and drained
2   tablespoons miso

Cook beans in pressure cooker with bay leaf and kombu in water until tender; drain.

Meanwhile, lightly brush the bottom of soup pot with oil; place over high heat. Sauté onions and garlic with salt 3 to minutes or until translucent. Add vegetable stock, parsley, and tomatoes, if desired; cover and simmer over low heat 30 minutes. Add celery, zucchini, and carrot; simmer 15 minutes. Stir in oregano, basil, cooked macaroni and beans. Scoop out about ½ cup soup; pour over miso and stir until dissolve. Stir into soup; simmer over low heat 3 minutes. Ladle into bowls.

Adzuki Bean Soup

1   cup dried adzuki beans, rinsed and drained
1   strip kombu
1   large yellow onion, chopped
1   large carrot, cut into matchsticks
1   stalk celery, chopped
6   cups water
1   bay leaf
1   teaspoon basil (optional)
1   pinch sea salt
½   cup sautéed sliced mushrooms (optional)
1   tablespoon miso, or to taste
¼   cup chopped green onions OR parsley, for garish

Place kombu on bottom of large pressure cooker; add beans, yellow onion, carrot, celery, water, bay leaf, and basil. Bring to pressure over high heat; reduce heat to low and cook 45 minutes. Stir in salt and mushrooms. Scoop out about ½ cup soup; pour over miso and stir until dissolved. Stir into soup; simmer over low heat 3 minutes. Ladle into bowls; garnish each serving with green onions.

Chickpea Potage

1   cup dried chickpeas, rinsed and soaked OR parboiled
5   cups Basic Vegetable Stock (recipe page 60) OR water
1   strip kombu
1   bay leaf
    Olive oil
1   large onion, chopped
2   cloves garlic, minced
½   teaspoon sea salt
½   teaspoon cumin
2   teaspoons tahini (optional)
1   tablespoon miso
¼   cup chopped fresh dill weed OR parsley

Place chick peas, vegetable stock, kombu, and bay leaf in pressure cooker.

recipe continued following page

Bring to pressure over high heat; reduce heat to low and cook 1 hour. Remove bay leaf and kombu.

Meanwhile, lightly the heated bottom of soup pot with oil; place over high heat. Sauté onion and garlic with salt 3 to 4 minutes; cover and reduce heat to low. Cook 4 to 5 minutes or until onion is translucent. Stir in chickpeas with vegetable stock, cumin, and tahini, if desired.

Purée soup in batches in blender or food processor; return to pot. Simmer 3 to 4 minutes over low heat. Scoop out about ½ cup soup; pour over miso and stir until dissolved. Stir into soup; simmer over low heat 3 to 4 minutes. Ladle into bowls; garnish each serving with dill weed.

Chickpea Soup

1   cup dried chickpeas, rinsed and presoaked
5   cups water
    Olive oil
1   large onion, chopped
2 - 4 cloves garlic, crushed
¼   teaspoon cumin
¼   teaspoon mustard powder
1   pinch sea salt, or to taste
¼   cup chopped fresh cilantro
1   tablespoon miso, or to taste

Place chickpeas and water in pressure cooker; bring to pressure over high heat. Reduce heat to low; cook for 1 hour.

Meanwhile, lightly coat the bottom of large skillet with oil; place over high heat. Sauté onion and garlic 4 to 5 minutes or until golden; remove from heat.

Stir onion mixture, cumin, mustard, and salt into chickpea mixture. Simmer over low heat 20 minutes. Stir in cilantro; simmer 15 minutes. Scoop out about ½ cup soup; pour over miso and stir until dissolved. Stir into soup; simmer over low heat 5 minutes. Ladle into bowls.

Split Pea Soup

4   cups unsalted Basic Vegetable Stock (recipe page 60)
     OR water
1   cup split peas
1   large onion, finely chopped
1   large carrot, cut into matchsticks
1   strip kombu
1   stalk celery, chopped
1   bay leaf
1   pinch sea salt
2   tablespoons miso, or to taste
     Herbed Croutons (recipe page 61)

Place all ingredients except salt, miso, and croutons in pressure cooker. Bring to pressure over high heat; reduce heat and cook 30 minutes or until creamy in consistency. Stir in salt. Scoop out about ½ cup soup; pour over miso and stir until dissolved. Stir into soup; simmer over low heat 3 minutes. Ladle into bowls; garnish each serving with Herbed Croutons.

Black Bean Soup

1   cup dried black beans, rinsed, presoaked, and drained
1   strip kombu
1   bay leaf
4   cups Basic Vegetable Stock (recipe page 60) OR water
     Olive oil
1   large yellow onion, finely chopped
2 - 3 cloves garlic
1   stalk celery, chopped
1   large carrot, cut into matchsticks
2   green onions, chopped
3   tablespoons orange juice (optional)
1   teaspoon cumin
½   teaspoon oregano
1   pinch sea salt
2   tablespoons miso, or to taste
¼   cup chopped fresh cilantro
     Lemon wedges, for garnish

recipe continued following page

Place beans, kombu, bay leaf, and vegetable stock in pressure cooker. Bring to pressure over high heat; reduce heat to low and cook 45 minutes.

Meanwhile, lightly coat heated bottom of large skillet with oil; place over high heat. Sauté yellow onion and garlic 3 to 4 minutes until onion is translucent. Stir in celery, carrot, and green onions; sauté 3 minutes. Remove from heat; stir into bean mixture with orange juice, cumin, oregano, and salt. Simmer over low heat 15 minutes. Scoop out about ½ cup soup; pour over miso and stir until dissolved. Stir into soup; simmer over low heat 5 minutes. Ladle into bowls; garnish each serving with cilantro and a lemon wedge.

Navy Bean and Sweet Corn Soup

1   cup dried navy beans, rinsed, presoaked, and drained
1   bay leaf
1   strip kombu
5   cups Basic Vegetable Stock (recipe page 60) OR water
     Olive oil
1   large onion, chopped
1   ear sweet corn
1   stalk celery, chopped
¼   teaspoon thyme
1   pinch sea salt
1   tablespoon miso
¼   cup chopped fresh parsley

Place beans, bay leaf, kombu, and water in pressure cooker. Bring to pressure over high heat; reduce heat to low and cook 40 minutes.

Meanwhile, lightly coat the bottom of large skillet with oil; place over high heat. Sauté onion 3 to 4 minutes or until translucent. Stir in celery; reduce heat to low. Cut corn off cob; discard cob. Stir kernels into skillet; sauté 3 minutes. Remove from heat; stir into bean mixture with thyme and salt; simmer 15 minutes over low heat. Scoop out about ½ cup soup; pour over miso and stir until dissolved. Stir into soup; simmer over low heat 3 minutes. Ladle into bowls; garnish each serving with parsley.

Yellow Split Pea Potage

1   cup dried yellow split peas, picked over, rinsed, and drained
4   cups Basic Vegetable Stock (recipe page 60) OR water
1   bay leaf
1   strip kombu
¼   teaspoon tumeric
    Olive oil
1   large onion, finely chopped
1   pinch sea salt, or to taste
2 - 3 cloves garlic, crushed
1   leek, washed thoroughly and chopped
1   tablespoon grated fresh ginger root
½   teaspoon thyme
1   tablespoon shoyu
1   tablespoon miso
¼   cup chopped fresh parsley

Place yellow split peas, vegetable stock, bay leaf, kombu, and tumeric in pressure cooker. Bring to pressure over high heat; reduce heat to low and cook 40 minutes.

Meanwhile, lightly coat the bottom of large skillet with oil; place over high heat. Sauté onion 3 to 4 minutes or until translucent; sprinkle with salt and cover. Reduce heat to low and cook 3 minutes. Stir in garlic, leek, ginger, and thyme; sauté 5 minutes. Remove from heat; stir into pea mixture with shoyu. Simmer over low heat 5 minutes. Scoop out about ½ cup soup; pour over miso and stir until dissolved. Stir into soup; simmer over low heat 3 minutes. Ladle into bowls; garnish each serving with parsley.

Creamy Cucumber Soup

1   large onion, chopped
    Olive oil
2   cloves garlic, crushed
1   pinch sea salt
4   cups Basic Vegetable Stock (recipe page 60) OR water
²/₃ cup old-fashioned rolled oats (not instant)
4   to 6 Kirby cucumbers OR 2 large cucumbers, peeled, seeded, and chopped, divided

recipe continued following page

1   pinch white pepper
2   tablespoons miso
1   tablespoon chopped fresh dill weed

Lightly coat the bottom of soup pot with oil; place over high heat. Sauté onion and garlic with salt 3 to 4 minutes or until translucent. Add vegetable stock and oats; bring to a boil. Reduce heat and simmer, covered, 15 minutes.

Purée with about ¼ cup chopped cucumber in batches in blender or food processor; return to pot. Stir in white pepper, dill weed, and remaining chopped cucumbers. Scoop out about ½ cup soup; pour over miso and stir until dissolved. Stir into soup. Refrigerate; serve chilled.

Curried Carrot Bisque

1   large onion, chopped
    Olive oil
1   pinch sea salt
4   cups Basic Vegetable Stock (recipe page 60) OR water
3   large carrots, sliced
2/3 cup old-fashioned rolled oats (not instant)
½   teaspoon curry powder
1   tablespoon grated fresh ginger root
2   tablespoons miso, or to taste

Lightly coat the bottom of soup pot with oil; place over high heat. Sauté onion 3 to 4 minutes or until translucent; reduce heat to low. Sprinkle with salt; cover and cook 4 minutes. Add vegetable stock, carrots, oats, and curry powder; bring to a boil over high heat. Reduce heat to low and simmer, covered, for 10 minutes.

Purée soup in batches in blender or food processor; return to pot. Scoop out about ½ cup soup; pour over miso and stir until dissolved. Stir into soup with ginger. Serve either hot or chilled.

Variation: Carrot Bisque with Dill. Prepare soup as above, eliminating curry and ginger. Just before serving, stir in 2 tablespoons chopped fresh dill weed.

Dispensation food: for those requiring a transition from a meat-based diet or for specific health needs—not necessary for complete nutrition.

Basic Fish Stock

1   3-pound white fish, bones and head only
6-7 cups water
2   stalks celery with leaves, chopped
1   large onion, cut into wedges
½   cup chopped fresh parsley
2   bay leaves
1½ teaspoons sea salt
⅛   teaspoon black pepper

Bring fish trimmings and water to a boil in soup pot over high heat. Skim surface of water with spoon to remove any foam. Add celery, onion, parsley, bay leaves, salt and pepper; reduce heat to medium. Cover and simmer 30 to 40 minutes. Strain stock; refrigerate until ready to use.

Kombu and Bonito Flake Soup

1   large strip kombu
4   cups cold water
1   (.175-ounce) package loosely packed bonito flakes (about ½ cup)
1   tablespoon shoyu
1-2 tablespoons brown rice miso
1   tablespoon sweet white miso
    Garnishes such as watercress, steamed carrot flowers, noodles, tofu, chopped green onions, steamed pea pods

Place kombu with water in soup pot; bring to a boil over high heat. Remove from heat. Remove kombu with tongs; reserve for another use. Add bonito flakes to pot; do not stir. Let stand for 3 minutes.

Line a sieve with cheesecloth; strain soup. Squeeze out cheesecloth by gathering edges and twisting to extract any liquid or by pressing the bonito flakes in strainer with the back of a spoon. Discard bonito flakes. Heat stock over medium heat in soup pot; stir in shoyu. Scoop out about ½ cup soup; pour over both misos and stir until dissolved. Stir into soup; simmer over low heat 3 minutes. Garnish as desired; serve hot.

Fish Dumpling Soup

Fish Dumplings (recipe follows)
1   large strip kombu
6   cups water
1   3-pound white fish, bones and head only (flesh reserved for Fish Dumplings)
¼   cup chopped fresh parsley
1   large yellow onion, quartered
1   leek, thoroughly rinsed and chopped
2   cloves garlic, crushed
1 - 2 teaspoons ginger juice, squeezed from grated fresh ginger root
1   pinch sea salt, or to taste
¼   teaspoon pepper
1 - 2 tablespoon miso
3   tablespoons chopped green onion

Prepare Fish Dumplings; set aside.

Simmer kombu, fish bones, parsley, and yellow onion in water in soup pot over medium heat 25 minutes. Strain through cheesecloth; discard bones and vegetables. Return stock to pot; add leek, garlic, ginger juice, salt, and pepper. Simmer over low heat 3 minutes. Drop in dumplings; simmer 5 minutes. Scoop out about ½ cup soup; pour over miso and stir until dissolved. Stir into soup; simmer over low heat 3 minutes. Ladle soup and dumplings into bowls; garnish each serving with green onion.

FISH DUMPLINGS

Reserved flesh from 3-pound white fish, ground
2   green onions, minced
1   tablespoon grated fresh ginger root
1   teaspoon sea salt
1   tablespoon shoyu
1   pinch white pepper

Combine all ingredients in a large bowl. Form into 1-inch balls.

Provincial Fish Soup

2 pounds white fish or snapper, cut into fillets, bones reserved
10 cups water, divided
¼ teaspoon sea salt
½ cup chopped fresh parsley
2 bay leaves
Olive oil
2 large onions, chopped
4 cloves garlic, crushed
1 leek, thoroughly rinsed and chopped
2 branches fresh fennel (optional)
½ teaspoon thyme
1 16-ounce can peeled Italian plum tomatoes, drained
¼ teaspoon grated orange peel
2 tablespoons sake or white wine
1 pinch saffron
Herbed Croutons (recipe page 61), optional

Bring fish bones, 6 cups water, salt, parsley, and bay leaves to a boil in large soup pot over high heat. Reduce heat to low and simmer 30 minutes.

Meanwhile, coat the bottom of large skillet with oil; place over high heat. Sauté onions, garlic, leek, fennel, and thyme 2 to 3 minutes; reduce heat to low and cover. Cook 5 minutes or until translucent. Remove from heat; set aside.

Line sieve with cheesecloth; strain fish stock. Discard bones and herbs. Return stock to pot; stir in remaining 4 cups water, onion mixture, tomatoes, and orange peel. Bring to a boil over high heat; reduce heat to low and simmer 20 minutes or until soup is reduced by ¼ volume. Remove orange peel with metal spoon; stir in saffron and fish fillets. Simmer 8 to 10 minutes. Purée soup in small batches in blender or food processor; strain back into pot. Simmer 5 minutes; ladle into bowls. Garnish each serving with Herbed Croutons, if desired.

GRAINS & PASTA

Basic Brown Rice

Tip: Always rinse rice with cool water in large bowl; drain in a strainer. Repeat process until water is almost clear (about 3 times).

To Pressure-Cook Rice: Combine rinsed brown rice, water, and sea salt in pressure cooker. (For each cup rice use 1½ cups water and 1 pinch sea salt.) Cover and bring to pressure over high heat. Reduce heat to low; cook 40 to 50 minutes. Remove from heat; allow pressure to drop completely before opening pot. Gently separate grains while scooping rice into large serving bowl. (Do not leave rice in pot to cool or condensation will alter the flavor and texture.)

To Boil Rice: Combine 1 cup brown rice, 2 cups water, and 1 pinch sea salt in large, heavy pot with tight-fitting lid. Bring to a boil over high heat; cover and reduce heat to low. Simmer 45 to 50 minutes. Remove from heat and let stand, covered, 5 minutes. Uncover and stir lightly to separate grains. Spread rice in serving bowl.

To Bake Rice: Preheat oven to 350°F. Toast 2 cups brown rice in large dry skillet over medium heat 5 minutes, or until fragrant, stirring frequently. Combine rice, 4 cups boiling water, and 1 pinch sea salt in glass casserole. Bake, covered, 45 to 50 minutes. Mix gently to separate grains; serve hot.

Vegetable Rice Pilaf and Stuffing

1	large onion, chopped
½	cup Basic Vegetable Stock (recipe page 60), divided
2	cloves garlic, crushed
1	large carrot, cut into matchsticks
1	stalk celery, chopped
½	pound mushrooms, sliced
2	tablespoons chopped fresh parsley
2	cups cooked long grain brown rice
2	cups cooked wheat berries
¼	teaspoon EACH: dried oregano and thyme
⅛	teaspoon dried sage
1	pinch sea salt, or to taste

Simmer onion in ¼ cup vegetable stock in large skillet over medium heat 5 minutes or until translucent. Stir in garlic, carrot, and celery; simmer 3 minutes. Add remaining stock and mushrooms; simmer 7 minutes or until mushrooms are cooked. Stir in parsley, rice, wheat berries, oregano, thyme, sage, and salt. Cover; cook over low heat 3 minutes. Serve hot as a pilaf or let cool and use as a stuffing for fish.

Rice with Almonds and Capers

Mustard Vinaigrette Dressing (recipe follows)
2   cups long grain brown rice
4   cups Basic Vegetable Stock (recipe page 60) OR water
2   bay leaves
1/8 teaspoon sea salt (optional)
1/3 cup dry roasted slivered almonds
2   tablespoons capers, drained
2   green onions, finely chopped
1   teaspoon dried oregano

Prepare Mustard Vinaigrette Dressing; set aside.

Bring rice, vegetable stock, bay leaves, and salt to a boil in large covered pot over high heat. Reduce heat; simmer 40 minutes. Carefully remove bay leaves; discard. Drain off any excess liquid. Scoop rice into large serving bowl; gently separate grains. Lightly toss rice with almonds, capers, green onion, oregano, and desired amount of dressing. Serve warm.

MUSTARD VINAIGRETTE DRESSING

6   tablespoons olive oil
2   tablespoons fresh lime OR lemon juice
1   tablespoon brown rice vinegar
2   teaspoons prepared yellow mustard
1   clove garlic, crushed
½   teaspoon sea salt
½   teaspoon Japanese-style citrus hot sauce

Combine all ingredients in jar with tight-fitting lid; cover and shake vigorously.

Brown Rice Salad

Orange-Ginger Vinaigrette (recipe page 155)
1   cup long grain brown rice
2   cups Basic Vegetable Stock (recipe page 60) OR water
1   bay leaf
1   medium bunch broccoli, cut into florets and stems sliced
1   red bell pepper, cored, seeded, and sliced
4   green onions, finely chopped
1   stalk celery, finely chopped
1/3 cup slivered toasted almonds
1/4 cup sliced black olives (optional)
2   tablespoons chopped fresh flat leaf parsley

Prepare Orange-Ginger Vinaigrette; set aside.

Bring rice, vegetable stock, and bay leaf to a boil in medium pot over high heat; reduce heat to low. Cover and simmer 45 minutes. Remove from heat, drain excess water, and allow rice to cool to room temperature; set aside.

Meanwhile, bring about 1 inch of water to a rolling boil in large pot with steam basket. Place broccoli in basket and steam, 3 to 5 minutes or until bright green and slightly tender. Remove broccoli from pot and rinse with cool water to stop the cooking process. Toss rice with broccoli and remaining salad ingredients in large serving bowl. Toss with desired amount of dressing; refrigerate.

Saffron Brown Rice

Olive oil
1   large yellow onion, thinly sliced into half moons
1¼ cups long grain or basmati brown rice
1   clove garlic, crushed
2   cups Basic Vegetable Stock (recipe page 60) OR water
1   pinch saffron
1   teaspoon lemon zest (outermost part of peel)
1/3 cup green peas
1/3 cup cooked chickpeas or adukis
1/4 cup sliced black olives (optional)
3   green onions, sliced into 1-inch pieces

Lightly coat the bottom of large skillet with oil; place over high heat. Sauté yellow onion 3 to 4 minutes or until translucent; reduce heat to low. Stir in rice and garlic; cook 3 minutes. Add vegetable stock; bring to a boil. Sir in saffron and lemon zest. Cover and simmer 30 minutes. Stir in green peas, chickpeas, olives (if desired), and green onions. Cover and cook 15 minutes. Spoon into large serving bowl; gently separate grains with tines of fork. Garnish with parsley, if desired.

Saffron Rice Salad

Olive Oil Vinaigrette (recipe follows)
1 large yellow onion, finely chopped
Olive oil
1 cup brown rice
2 cups Basic Vegetable Stock (recipe page 60) OR water
1 pinch saffron
1½ cups green peas
1 red bell pepper, cored, seeded, and chopped (optional)
¼ cup sliced black olives (optional)
2 green onions, chopped

Prepare Olive Oil Vinaigrette; set aside.

Lightly coat heated bottom of large skillet with oil; place over high heat. Sauté yellow onion 3 to 4 minutes or until translucent; reduce heat to low. Stir in rice, vegetable stock, saffron, and peas. Cover and simmer 40 minutes; remove from heat and let cool. Stir in bell pepper, olives (if desired), green onions, and vinaigrette. Spoon into large serving bowl; serve warm.

OLIVE OIL VINAIGRETTE

⅓ cup olive oil
3 tablespoons brown rice vinegar
1 clove garlic, minced
1 pinch sea salt

Combine all ingredients in jar with tight-fitting lid; cover and shake vigorously. **Note:** This recipe can also be refrigerated and served chilled as a refreshing summer salad.

Rice Timbales

1   medium onion, minced
     Olive oil
1   pinch sea salt
1   cup short grain brown rice
1   ounce dried mushrooms (any variety), soaked and
     drained according to package directions (liquid
     reserved), chopped
2 ½ cups Basic Vegetable Stock (recipe page 57) OR water
¼   cup chopped fresh parsley
1   pinch pepper
     Steamed kale leaves (optional)

Lightly coat heated bottom of large pot with oil; place over high heat. Sauté onion 3 to 4 minutes or until translucent; sprinkle with salt. Stir in rice, mushrooms, soaking liquid, and vegetable stock; reduce heat to low. Cover and simmer 45 minutes or until liquid is absorbed. Stir in parsley and pepper. Firmly pack rice mixture into 8 lightly oiled ramekins or molds; let stand 5 minutes. Unmold onto serving platter covered with steamed kale leaves, if desired. Serve immediately.

Basmati Rice with Black-Eyed Peas

2   cups brown basmati rice
4   cups Basic Vegetable Stock (recipe page 57) OR water,
     divided
½   cup dried black-eyed peas, rinsed, presoaked, and
     drained
½   strip kombu
     Olive oil
1   large onion, finely chopped
2   cloves garlic, crushed
1   bay leaf
1   teaspoon cumin
¼   teaspoon tumeric
1   pinch EACH: sea salt and pepper
1   tablespoon brown rice vinegar
2   tablespoons chopped fresh cilantro or parsley

In medium pot combine rice and 3 cups vegetable stock; place over high heat. Bring to a boil; cover and reduce heat to low. Simmer 45 minutes or until tender.

In another medium pot combine peas, bay leaf, kombu, and 1 cup vegetable stock; place over high heat. Bring to a boil; cover and reduce heat to low. Simmer 45 minutes or until tender but whole. Drain; carefully remove kombu.

Lightly coat heated bottom of large skillet with oil; place over high heat. Sauté onion with garlic 3 to 4 minutes or until translucent; reduce heat to low. Stir in cumin, tumeric, salt, and pepper; remove from heat.

In large serving bowl stir together rice, peas, onion mixture, and vinegar. Garnish with cilantro; serve warm.

Wild Rice Pilaf

Orange-Dijon Dressing (recipe follows)
1   cup wild rice
4½ cups Basic Vegetable Stock (recipe page 60) OR water,
     divided
1   cup long grain brown rice
½   cup pecans, chopped
4   green onions, thinly sliced
½   cup chopped parsley

Prepare Orange-Dijon Dressing; set aside.

In medium pot, bring wild rice and 2¼ cups vegetable stock to a boil over high heat. Cover and reduce heat to low; simmer 40 minutes or until tender.

Meanwhile, in another medium pot, bring brown rice and 2¼ cups vegetable stock to a boil over high heat. Cover and reduce heat to low; simmer 40 minutes or until tender.

In large serving bowl, stir together, wild rice, brown rice, pecans, green onions, parsley, and dressing. Serve warm.

Orange Dijon Dressing

1   teaspoon orange zest (outermost part of peel)
5   tablespoons fresh orange juice
4   tablespoons olive oil
½-1 teaspoon sea salt, or to taste
1   teaspoon prepared dijon mustard
⅛ teaspoon pepper

Combine all ingredients in jar with tight-fitting lid; cover and shake vigorously.

Baked Rice Pilaf

1   cup dried fine noodles (such as semen), broken into
    small pieces
    Canola oil
3   cups short grain brown rice
5   cups boiling Basic Vegetable Stock (recipe page 60) OR
    water
1   pinch sea salt
¾ cup dry-roasted sunflower meats, sesame seeds, OR
    slivered almonds

Preheat oven to 350°F.

Lightly coat heated bottom of large skillet with oil; place over medium heat. Saute noodles until golden; stir in rice and toast 3 to 4 minutes or until fragrant, stirring often. Remove from heat.

lace rice-noodle mixture in glass baking dish with cover; carefully stir in boiling vegetable stock and salt. Cover and bake 45 minutes. Just before serving, stir in sunflower meats.

Sweet Brown Rice Dumplings

2   cups short grain brown rice
4   cups water

¼   cup EACH brown rice syrup, toasted sesame seeds
     (optional)
1   pinch sea salt

Combine rice, water, syrup, and salt in pressure cooker; bring to pressure over high heat. Reduce heat to low and cook 45 minutes. Allow pressure to drop completely before removing cover.

Spoon rice into large wooden or unbreakable bowl. Using wooden pestle or mallet, pound rice until grains are half-crushed, dampening bottom of pestle with water as necessary to prevent sticking. With wet hands, form pounded rice into balls or ovals. Roll dumplings in roasted sesame seeds, sweet bean paste, rice syrup and kinako, ground chestnuts, or another coating of your choice, if desired. Or, simmer plain in a clear soup a few minutes as dumplings.

Rice Patties

3 ½ cups leftover cooked brown rice
3   tablespoons fresh grated onion
1   egg, lightly beaten
1   tablespoon whole wheat bread crumbs
1   small carrot, grated
½   teaspoon sea salt
¼   teaspoon dried oregano
     Canola oil
     Mushroom Kuzu Sauce (recipe page 157), optional

Steam rice to soften; let stand until cool enough to handle. Mash vigorously with back of fork until pasty. Combine with remaining ingredients except oil until well incorporated. Form into 2- to 3-inch patties.

Heat about 1 tablespoon oil in large skillet over medium heat. Cook 3 to 4 patties at a tiime until bottoms are golden, about 3 minutes. Turn with spatula and cook other sides until golden.

Remove to paper towel-lined platter; pat dry to remove excess oil. Keep warm; repeat with remaining patties. Serve with Mushroom Kuzu Sauce, if desired.

Vegetable-Fried Rice

2   cups broccoli florets, steamed until crisp-tender
    Canola oil
1   cup sliced mushrooms
4   green onions, finely chopped
1   teaspoon grated fresh ginger root
1   pinch sea salt
4   cups cooked brown rice
    Shoyu

Lightly coat heated bottom of large skillet with oil; stir in broccoli, mushrooms, green onions, and ginger. Sprinkle with sea salt and stir-fry 5 to 6 minutes or until crisp-tender.

Stir in rice; cover and cook 3 minutes over low heat. Season with shoyu to taste. Serve hot.

Variation: Substitute cooked millet or bulgur for rice.

Chickpea-Millet Patties

2   cups cooked chickpeas
1½   cups cooked millet
1   small onion, grated
1   medium carrot, grated
1   teaspoon cumin
1   pinch EACH: sea salt and pepper, or to taste
     Canola oil
¼   cup chopped fresh parsley
     Basic Brown Sauce (recipe page 158), optional

Mash chickpeas with fork in large bowl; stir in millet until combined. Stir in onion, carrot, cumin, salt, and pepper. Form into 3- to 4-inch patties.

Lightly coat the bottom of a large skillet with oil; place over medium heat. Cook 3 to 4 patties at a time until bottoms are golden, about 3 minutes. Turn with spatula and cook other sides until golden. Remove to paper towel-lined platter. Keep warm; repeat with remaining patties. Garnish with parsley and top with Basic Brown Sauce, if desired.

Millet with Sautéed Vegetables

1   cup millet, rinsed and drained
     Olive oil
1   medium onion, halved and sliced into half-rings
2   cloves garlic, minced
1   large carrot, cut into matchsticks
1   stalk celery, chopped
1   tablespoon grated fresh ginger root
2½ cups Basic Vegetable Stock (recipe page 57) OR water
2   teaspoons shoyu or ⅛ teaspoon sea salt

Dry roast millet in large skillet 4 to 5 minutes or until fragrant, stirring often. Remove millet from skillet; set aside.

Lightly coat bottom of same skillet with oil; place over high heat. Sauté onion with garlic 3 to 4 minutes or until translucent; reduce heat to low. Stir in carrot, celery, and ginger; sauté 3 minutes. Stir in millet, vegetable stock, and shoyu. Cover; simmer 20 minutes or until liquid is absorbed. Serve hot.

Millet Stew

1   cup millet, rinsed and drained
5   cups water
¼   teaspoon sea salt
1   teaspoon olive oil
1   large onion, chopped
1   large carrot, cut into matchsticks
5   dried shiitake mushrooms, soaked and drained according
     to package directions, knobby stems removed, sliced
1   bay leaf
¼   teaspoon thyme or basil
2   tablespoons shoyu
     Chopped fresh parsley, optional

Dry roast millet in large skillet 4 to 5 minutes or until fragrant, stirring often. Remove from heat; set aside.

Bring water to a rolling boil in large soup pot; stir in millet, salt, oil, onion,

Recipe continued on following page

carrot, mushrooms, bay leaf, and thyme. Cover and simmer over low heat
40 minutes. Just before serving, stir in shoyu. Spoon into bowls; garnish
each serving with parsley, if desired.

Saffron Millet Pilaf

1   cup millet, rinsed and drained
3   cups Basic Vegetable Stock (recipe page 60) OR water
1   pinch saffron
1   large yellow onion, chopped
3   green onions, chopped
2   tablespoons sliced black olives (optional)
2   cloves garlic, crushed
1   tablespoon fresh lemon juice
1/3 cup fresh green peas
1   pinch sea salt, or to taste

Dry roast millet in large skillet 4 to 5 minutes or until fragrant, stirring often.
Remove from heat; set aside.

Bring vegetable stock to a rolling boil in large soup pot; stir in millet, saffron,
yellow onion, green onions, olives (if desired), garlic, and lemon juice. Cover
and simmer over low heat 40 minutes or until liquid is absorbed. Stir in
peas; steam 2 minutes. Remove from heat; serve immediately.

Wheatberry and Barley Salad

    Lime-Ginger Dressing (recipe following)
1   cup pearled barley, rinsed and drained
½   cup wheatberries, rinsed, presoaked, and drained
3¼ cups Basic Vegetable Stock (recipe page 60) OR water,
    divided
1   pinch sea salt
    Sliced black olives (optional)

Prepare Lime-Ginger Dressing; set aside.

In large pot, bring barley and 2¼ cups vegetable stock to a boil; cover and
simmer 20 minutes. Drain off any excess liquid.

Meanwhile, in another large pot, bring wheatberries, remaining 1 cup vegetable stock, and salt to a boil; cover and simmer 45 minutes or until tender. Drain off any excess liquid.

In large bowl, toss barley and wheatberries with dressing; let cool to room temperature. Serve in individual lettuce cups; garnish with sliced olives, if desired.

Lime-Ginger Dressing

6 tablespoons olive or canola oil
3 tablespoons lime juice
1 teaspoon ginger juice
2 tablespoons chopped lemon grass (if available)
¼ teaspoon sea salt, or to taste

Blend all ingredients.

Wheatberry and Rice Pilaf

   Olive oil
1 large onion, finely chopped
1 pinch sea salt, or to taste
1 cup wheatberries, presoaked and drained
½ cup long grain brown rice
2½ cups Basic Vegetable Stock (recipe page 60) OR water
¼ teaspoon dried thyme
1 tablespoon shoyu
¼ cup toasted slivered almonds

Lightly coat the bottom of large soup pot with oil; place over high heat. Sauté onion 3 to 4 minutes or until translucent; sprinkle with sea salt. Cover and reduce heat to low; cook 3 minutes. Stir in wheatberries, rice, vegetable stock, and thyme. Cover; simmer 45 minutes. Stir in shoyu. Garnish with almond slices; serve hot.

Basic Bulgur

1   cup bulgur
2   cups Basic Vegetable Stock (recipe page 61) OR water
¼   teaspoon sea salt

Dry roast bulgur in large skillet over medium heat 3 to 4 minutes or until fragrant, stirring often. Remove bulgur to large glass bowl; let cool to room temperature.

Bring vegetable stock and salt to a boil; pour over roasted bulgur. Cover; let stand 30 minutes. Fluff lightly with fork before serving.

Homestyle Bulgur

2   cups boiling Basic Vegetable Stock (recipe page 61) OR water
1   cup bulgur
2   green onions, finely chopped
1   clove garlic, minced
1   pinch sea salt
    Minced fresh parsley

Pour boiling vegetable stock over bulgur in large glass bowl; stir in green onions, garlic, and salt. Cover; let stand 30 minutes. Fluff lightly with fork; garnish with parsley.

Tabouli

2   cups boiling Basic Vegetable Stock (recipe page 61) OR water
1   cup bulgur
1   kirby cucumber, peeled, seeded, and chopped
½   cup chopped green onions (about 3)
1   large tomato, seeded, diced (optional)
½   cup chopped fresh parsley
¼   cup chopped fresh mint leaves

¼   cup fresh lemon juice
2   tablespoons olive oil
1   pinch sea salt, or to taste
    Lemon slices

Pour boiling vegetable stock over bulgur in large glass bowl. Cover; let stand
25 minutes. Mix in cucumber, green onions, tomato (if desired), parsley,
and mint. In small bowl, whisk together lemon juice, olive oil, and salt; pour
over bulgur-vegetable mixture. Toss until well combined; refrigerate. Serve
garnished with lemon slices.

Couscous Salad

4   cups Basic Vegetable Stock (recipe page 60) OR water
3   tablespoons olive oil, divided
2   cups couscous
½   teaspoon powdered ginger
¼   teaspoon saffron
3   green onions, finely chopped
1   large carrot, diced
1   stalk celery, finely chopped
¼   cup chopped fresh parsley
1   tablespoon brown vinegar
½   teaspoon sea salt
½   cup toasted pine nuts (optional)

Bring vegetable stock and 1 tablespoon oil to a boil in large soup pot over
high heat. Stir in couscous, ginger, and saffron; reduce heat to low. Simmer
10 minutes or until most of liquid is absorbed. Cover; remove from heat and
let stand 10 minutes. Stir in green onions, carrot, and celery. In small bowl
mix together parsley, vinegar, sea salt, and remaining 2 tablespoons oil; stir
into couscous mixture. Cover and refrigerate 3 hours. Just before serving,
stir in pine nuts, if desired.

Couscous-Red Pepper Salad

      Lemon-Olive Oil Dressing (recipe follows)
2   cups cooked couscous
2   cups cooked chickpeas
6   green onions, minced
3   cucumber-pickles, peeled, seeded, and diced
1   red bell pepper, cored, seeded, and chopped

Prepare Lemon-Olive Oil Dressing; set aside.

In large serving bowl, combine all salad ingredients. Pour dressing over; mix thoroughly. Serve chilled.

LEMON OLIVE-OIL DRESSING

4   tablespoons olive oil
3   tablespoons fresh lemon juice
1   clove garlic, minced
½   teaspoon dried mustard powder
½   teaspoon sea salt

Combine all ingredients in jar with tight-fitting lid; shake vigorously.

Couscous with Vegetables and Seitan

1   large onion, cut into 8 wedges
      Olive oil
2   cloves garlic, crushed
1½ teaspoons tumeric
½   teaspoon EACH: cumin and powdered ginger
1   pinch saffron
4   cups Basic Vegetable Stock (recipe page 60) OR water
2   tablespoons shoyu
1   large carrot, sliced on a diagonal
2   zucchini, sliced on a diagonal
1   red bell pepper, cored, seeded, and sliced

¼ cup chopped fresh cilantro
2 cups cooked couscous
2 cups sliced sautéed seitan

Lightly coat the bottom of soup pot with oil; place over high heat. Sauté onion and garlic over high heat 4 minutes or until translucent; reduce heat to low. Stir in tumeric, cumin, ginger, vegetable stock, and shoyu; simmer 10 minutes. Stir in carrots, zucchini, red pepper, and cilantro; simmer 5 minutes. Carefully scoop out 1 cup stock; reserve. Drain vegetables in large colander.

Spoon cooked couscous onto a large serving platter; make a well in center. Spoon cooked vegetables into depression; top with sautéed seitan. Pass reserved stock to pour as desired over vegetables and couscous.

Chapatis (Pan-Grilled Flatbreads)

2 cups whole wheat flour
¼ teaspoon sea salt
¼ teaspoon curry powder (optional)
3 tablespoons olive oil
¼ cup lukewarm water

In large bowl, combine flour, salt, and curry powder, if desired. Cut in 3 tablespoons oil with pastry blender or 2 knives until fine crumbs form. Slowly pour in water, kneading thoroughly until dough is smooth and elastic, about 5 minutes. Cover and allow dough to rest at room temperature 45 to 60 minutes.

Separate dough into about 16 equal-sized balls. Roll out 2 balls between 2 sheets of waxed paper with rolling pin into about 5-inch circles. Lightly brush top of one circle with oil; place second round over. Press circles together to seal; cover with a damp cloth. Repeat with remaining dough balls.

Roll out 1 dough circle into a 9-inch round. Lightly oil heavy griddle or skillet; place over high heat. Cook until circle blisters and puffs up; flip with spatula and cook other side until golden. Remove from griddle; cover and keep warm. Repeat with remaining dough circles. Serve with a bean dip or as a side dish to broiled fish.

Polenta, Plain and Simple

3 ½ cups water
¼ - ½ teaspoon sea salt
1   cup corn grits
1   teaspoon olive oil

Bring water and salt to a boil in large pot over high heat. Gradually stir in corn grits; add oil, stirring frequently with wire whisk to prevent lumps from forming. Reduce heat to low; cover and simmer 15 to 20 minutes, stirring occasionally. Serve hot, sprinkled with toasted sesame or pumpkin seeds. Or, refrigerate until solid, cut into slices, and grill on a lightly oiled skillet until golden. Top with fruit preserves or syrup.

Polenta with Mushrooms

POLENTA
3 ½ cups water OR Basic Vegetable Stock (recipe page 60)
¼ - ½ teaspoon sea salt
1   cup corn grits
1   teaspoon olive oil
¼   teaspoon pepper

MUSHROOM TOPPING
     Olive oil
½   pound mushrooms, thinly sliced
1   clove garlic, crushed
½   teaspoon dried basil
¼   teaspoon thyme
¼   teaspoon dried rosemary
1   pinch black pepper
2   tablespoons dry white wine
1   teaspoon shoyu
     Chopped fresh parsley

For Polenta, bring water and sea salt to a boil in large pot over high heat. Gradually stir in corn grits; add oil and pepper, stirring frequently with wire whisk to prevent lumps from forming. Reduce heat to low; cover and simmer 15 to 20 minutes, stirring occasionally. Spoon into large serving bowl.

For Mushroom Topping, lightly brush the bottom of large skillet with oil; place over high heat. Sauté mushrooms 5 minutes or until tender; stir in basil, thyme, rosemary, and black pepper. Reduce heat to medium; sauté 2 minutes. Stir in wine and shoyu; cook 1 minute. Spoon over polenta; garnish with parsley. Serve immediately.

Polenta with Carrot Sauce

Polenta, Plain and Simple (recipe page 98)
3 large carrots, sliced
Olive oil
1. large onion, chopped
1 clove garlic, crushed
1 pinch sea salt, or to taste
1½ teaspoons miso
½ teaspoon dried basil
½ teaspoon garlic powder
¼ teaspoon dried oregano
1 pinch pepper

Prepare Polenta, Plain and Simple; keep warm.

For Carrot Sauce, steam carrots until fork-tender. Set aside. Lightly coat heated bottom of large skillet with oil; place over high heat. Sauté onion and garlic 4 minutes or until translucent; remove from heat. Purée carrots with onion mixture, salt, miso, basil, garlic powder, oregano, and pepper in blender of food processor until smooth; spoon over cooked polenta. Serve with Refried Beans (recipe page 108).

Cornbread

¼ cup canola oil
1 corn flour
½ cup corn grits
½ cup whole wheat pastry flour
1 tablespoon baking powder
¼ teaspoon sea salt

recipe continued on following page

1¼   cups vanilla-flavored soy milk
6   tablespoons brown rice syrup
1   tablespoon maple syrup (optional)
1   egg, lightly beaten OR egg substitute

Preheat oven to 400°F. Lightly coat 9-inch square baking pan with oil.

In large bowl, combine corn flour, corn grits, flour, baking powder, and salt; make a well in the center. In medium bowl, beat soy milk, ¼ cup canola oil, rice syrup, maple syrup (if desired), and egg. Pour liquid mixture into depression in dry ingredients; mix only until just combined (do not overmix). Pour batter into prepared pan; bake 30 minutes or until toothpick inserted near center comes out clean. If necessary, cover pan with foil to prevent overbrowning. Serve warm with jam or honey.

Tofu Cornbread

1   cup corn grits
¾   cup whole wheat pastry flour
2½   teaspoons baking powder (non alum)
⅛   teaspoon sea salt
¼   cup soy milk or water
4   ounces silken tofu, puréed
4   tablespoons canola oil
4   tablespoons brown rice syrup
1   tablespoon maple syrup (optional)

Preheat oven to 350°F. Lightly oil 8 x 4-inch loaf pan.

In large bowl, mix together corn grits, flour, baking powder, and salt; form well in center. In medium bowl, beat together soy milk, puréed tofu, oil, rice syrup, and maple syrup, if desired. Pour liquid mixture into depression in dry ingredients; mix only until just combined (do not overmix). Pour batter into prepared pan; bake 40 minutes or until toothpick inserted near center comes out clean. If necessary, cover with foil to prevent overburning.

Buckwheat Salad

2   cups Basic Vegetable Stock (recipe page 60) OR water
1   cup unroasted buckwheat
2   small cucumbers, peeled, seeded, chopped
2   green onions, chopped
2   tablespoons minced fresh parsley
3-4 tablespoons sesame oil
2   tablespoons brown rice vinegar
2   tablespoons fresh lemon juice
2   tablespoons umesu (umeboshi "vinegar")

Bring vegetable stock to a boil in large pot over high heat; stir in buckwheat. Reduce heat to low; simmer 10 minutes until buckwheat is cooked but still firm. Drain; spread buckwheat on a cookie sheet to cool.

In large serving bowl, toss cooled buckwheat with remaining ingredients. Serve warm or chilled.

Buckwheat Tabouli

4   cups Basic Vegetable Stock (recipe page 60) OR water
2   cup unroasted buckwheat
½   cup lemon juice
¼   cup olive oil
2   tablespoons shoyu
¼   cup chopped fresh parsley
1   clove garlic, crushed
1   tablespoon minced fresh dill weed
½   teaspoon dried basil
2   green onions, chopped

Bring vegetable stock to a boil in large pot over high heat; stir in buckwheat. Reduce heat to low; simmer 10 minutes until buckwheat is cooked but still firm. Drain; spread buckwheat on a cookie sheet to cool. Transfer to large serving bowl.

Combine lemon juice, oil, and shoyu in small bowl. Stir in parsley, garlic, dill, and basil. Pour over buckwheat; stir in green onions and olives. Refrigerate; serve chilled.

Buckwheat Pilaf

1   cup unroasted buckwheat
2   cups Basic Vegetable Stock (recipe page 60) OR water
    sea salt, to taste
    Olive oil
5   green onions, chopped
1/3 cup chopped fresh parsley
1/3 cup roasted sunflower meats
    Shoyu

Dry roast buckwheat in large skillet over medium heat 3 minutes or until fragrant, stirring often. In large soup pot, bring vegetable stock to a boil over high heat; stir in salt. Stir in buckwheat; cover and reduce heat to low. Simmer 10 to 12 minutes; drain and spread buckwheat on cookie sheet to cool.

Meanwhile, lightly coat the bottom of large skillet with oil; place over medium heat. Sauté green onions 3 minutes; stir in parsley and buckwheat. Stir in sunflower meats; sprinkle with a few drops shoyu. Toss lightly and serve.

Basic Quinoa

1   cup quinoa
2   cups Basic Vegetable Stock (recipe page 60) OR water

Rinse quinoa in cool water, rubbing the grains gently between both hands. Drain; repeat.

In large soup pot, bring vegetable stock to a rolling boil over high heat. Stir in quinoa; reduce heat and simmer, covered, 20 minutes or until translucent. Pour off any excess liquid. Fluff lightly with fork.

Garden Quinoa Salad

1   cup quinoa, rinsed and drained
2   cups Basic Vegetable Stock (recipe page 60) OR water
3   tablespoons olive oil

½   cup cubed seitan (optional)
2   tablespoons fresh lime juice
¼ - ½ teaspoon sea salt, or to taste
5   green onions, minced
2   Kirby cucumbers, peeled, seeded, and chopped
2   stalks celery, chopped
3   tablespoons chopped fresh parsley
2   tablespoons chopped fresh cilantro
1   clove garlic, crushed
1   teaspoon grated fresh ginger root

In large soup pot, bring vegetable stock to a rolling boil over high heat. Stir in quinoa; reduce heat and simmer, covered, 20 minutes or until translucent. Pour off any excess liquid. Fluff with fork; spoon into large serving bowl and allow to cool to room temperature.

Wisk together olive oil, lime juice, and sea salt. Pour over cooled quinoa. Toss with seitan and remaining ingredients. Refrigerate; serve chilled.

Italian Quinoa Salad

3   cups cooked quinoa, at room temperature
4   green onions, chopped
½   cup chopped fresh fennel (bulb and fronds)
½   red bell pepper, cored, seeded, and chopped
⅓   cup sliced black olives (optional)
3   tablespoons minced fresh parsley
2 - 3 tablespoons olive oil
1½ tablespoons balsamic vinegar
1   pinch sea salt, or to taste
1   pinch black pepper, or to taste

Combine quinoa, green onions, fennel, bell pepper, olives (if desired), and parsley in large serving bowl; toss lightly.

Whisk together oil, vinegar, salt, and black pepper; pour over quinoa-vegetable mixture. Toss lightly; refrigerate. Serve chilled, mounded on steamed kale leaves, if desired.

Quinoa with Seitan

1   cup quinoa, ringed and drained
2   cups Basic Vegetable Stock (recipe page 60) OR water
2   tablespoons olive oil
1   large onion, chopped
1   clove garlic, crushed
½   teaspoon cumin
1   tablespoon brown rice vinegar
1   pinch sea salt, or to taste
8   ounces seitan, sliced into thin strips
¼   cup chopped fresh cilantro

Bring vegetable stock or water to a rolling boil over high heat. Stir in quinoa; reduce heat and simmer covered, 12 minutes or until translucent. Pour off any excess liquid. Fluff lightly with fork.

Meanwhile, coat the bottom of large skillet with oil; place over high heat. Saute onion and garlic 4 minutes or until translucent; reduce heat to low. Sprinkle with cumin; stir in quinoa and saute 3 minutes. Stir in vinegar and salt. Stir in seitan strips; cook 5 minutes, stirring occasionally. Spoon into large serving dish; garnish with cilantro. Serve immediately.

Saffron Quinoa

1   cup quinoa, rinsed and drained
2   cups Basic Vegetable Stock (recipe page 60) OR water
    Olive oil
1   large onion, chopped
1   clove garlic, crushed
1   pinch sea salt, or to taste
3   tablespoons dry white wine
⅛   teaspoon saffron
½   red bell pepper, cored, needed, and chopped
⅓   cup sliced black olives (optional)
¼   cup chopped fresh parsley

In large soup pot, bring vegetable stock to a rolling boil over high heat. Stir in quince; reduce heat and simmer, covered, 20 minutes or until translucent. Pour off any excess liquid. Fluff lightly with fork.

Meanwhile, coat the bottom of large skillet with oil; place over high heat. Sauté onion and garlic 4 minutes or until translucent; reduce heat to low. Sprinkle with salt; stir in wine, saffron, bell pepper, and olives (if desired). Simmer 5 minutes; stir in quinoa. Cook 3 minutes; spoon in large serving bowl. Garnish with parsley; serve immediately.

Basic Teff

3 cups water OR Basic Vegetable Stock (recipe page 61)
1 cup teff
1 pinch sea salt

In large soup pot, bring water to a rolling boil. Whisk in teff and salt; cover and reduce heat to low. Simmer 15 minutes, stirring occasionally to prevent lumps from forming. Serve hot, topped with toasted pumpkin seeds or syrup.

Teff Patties

2 cups cooked teff
¼ cup grated carrot
¼ cup chopped green onions
2 tablespoons grated fresh yellow onion
1 clove garlic, crushed
¼ teaspoon sea salt
   Canola oil

Combine teff, carrot, green onions, yellow onion, garlic, and salt in large bowl. Form mixture into ¼-inch thick patties.

Lightly coat heated bottom of large skillet with oil; place over medium heat. Cook teff patties, 2 or 3 at a time, 5 minutes per side or until golden brown. Serve in toasted pita pockets with dijon mustard and lettuce.

Injera

4 cups purified water or spring water
2 cups teff flour (brown, red, or white)
¼ teaspoon sea salt
   Canola oil

In large non-metallic bowl, thoroughly mix together water and teff. Cover; let stand at room temperature overnight. Pour off any excess water from top of batter; stir in sea salt.

Coat heated bottom of large skillet with oil; place over high heat. Using a ½-cup measure, pour batter into skillet. Tilt skillet to spread batter evenly into a large thin pancake. Reduce heat to low; cover and cook 4 minutes. Flip pancake carefully with large metal spatula; cook 30 seconds. Remove injera from skillet; cover and keep warm. Repeat with remaining batter. Use to wrap cooked beans or curried vegetables.

Basic Dried Pasta

2 quarts water
1 pinch sea salt
8 ounces dried udon or soba pasta

In large stock pot, bring water and salt to a rolling boil over high heat. Add pasta, fanning out to prevent sticking. Return to a boil; reduce heat to medium. Cook pasta 7 minutes for al dente, 9 minutes for soft (test pasta while cooking to determine desired firmness).

Drain pasta in colander; rinse with cool water. Use as desired.

Soba with Shiitake Broth

4 dried shiitake mushrooms, soaked and drained according
   to package directions (liquid reserved)
4 cups water, including water from mushrooms
1 - 2 tablespoons shoyu

1   tablespoon sweet miso
1   teaspoon fresh ginger juice
8   ounces dried soba, cooked and drained
2   tablespoons chopped green onion

Remove knobby stems from mushrooms; discard. Slice caps; set aside.

Add enough water to reserved soaking liquid to measure 4 cups; place in large soup pot over high heat. Add sliced mushrooms; bring to a boil. Reduce heat and simmer 10 minutes. Stir in shoyu. Scoop out about ½ cup broth; pour over miso and stir until dissolved. Stir into broth with ginger juice. Add soba and green onion; simmer 3 minutes. Ladle into bowls.

Soba with Kombu Broth

4   cups cold water
1   strip kombu
2- 3 tablespoons shoyu
1   tablespoon mirin
1   tablespoon grated fresh ginger root (optional)
1   sheet nori, toasted and cut into thin strips
8   ounces dried soba, cooked and drained
2   tablespoons chopped green onion

Place water and kombu in large soup pot; bring to a boil over high heat. Carefully remove kombu; reserve for another use. Reduce heat to low; stir in shoyu, mirin, ginger, and nori. Stir in noodles, simmer 5 minutes. Stir in green onion; ladle into bowls.

Udon Noodles with Carrot-Basil Sauce

3   large carrots, sliced
1   medium onion, chopped
2   cloves garlic, crushed
½   cup water
¼   cup chopped fresh basil
1   pinch sea salt

recipe continued on following page

miso to taste (approximately ½ teaspoon per cup of cooked vegtables)
8   ounces dried udon noodles, cooked and drained
1   tablespoon chopped fresh parsley

In large soup pot over high heat, bring carrots, onion, garlic, water, basil, and salt to a boil; reduce heat to low and simmer 15 minutes or until vegetables are tender. Purée vegetable-broth mixture with miso in blender or food processor; return to soup pot. Simmer 3 minutes, thinning with 1 to 2 tablespoons water, if necessary. Pour sauce over udon noodles in large serving bowl; garnish with parsley.

Noodle Pancakes

6   ounces dried vermicelli noodles, broken into small pieces, cooked, and drained
1   tablespoon shoyu
1   egg, lightly beaten, or egg replacer
5   dried shiitake mushrooms, soaked and drained according to package directions, knobby stems removed, caps sliced
4   green onions, minced
1   medium carrot, grated
    Canola oil

In large bowl, beat together shoyu and egg; stir in noodles, mushrooms, green onions, and carrot.

Lightly coat the bottom of large skillet with oil; place over medium heat. Pour about ½ cup batter into skillet; cook 3 minutes of until golden. Carefully flip pancake over with metal spatula; cook other side 2 minutes. Remove pancake to paper towel-lined platter; keep warm. Repeat with remaining batter. Serve hot with unsweetened apple sauce.

Gingered Pasta Salad

6   ounces dried soba noodles, cooked, and drained
2   cups broccoli florets, steamed until crisp-tender, cooled
¼   cup chopped green onions
6   black olives, sliced (optional)
4   red radishes, thinly sliced
4   tablespoons toasted sesame oil
3   tablespoons brown rice vinegar
3   tablespoons shoyu
1   tablespoon grated fresh ginger root
1   teaspoon mirin

In large bowl, combine soba, broccoli, green onions, black olives (if desired), and radishes. In small bowl, whisk together oil, vinegar, shoyu, ginger, and mirin. Pour over soba mixture; toss lightly. Serve warm.

Pasta with Peanut Sauce

¼   cup natural peanut butter
¼   cup water
2   tablespoons shoyu
2   tablespoons brown rice vinegar
2   cloves garlic, crushed
1   green onion, finely chopped
2   teaspoons grated fresh ginger root
2   teaspoons brown rice syrup
8   ounces dried somen or soba noodles, cooked and drained
    Tofu and Pea Pods (recipe follows)
2-3 tablespoons minced fresh cilantro

Blend all ingredients except pasta, Tofu and Pea Pods, and cilantro in blender or food processor until creamy. Add 1 to 2 tablespoons water, if necessary, for desired consistency. (Sauce can be covered and stored in refrigerated at this point for up to 2 weeks.) Warm over low heat in heavy saucepan until hot. Toss with soba in large serving bowl. Stir in Tofu and Pea Pods; garnish with cilantro. Serve warm or chill as a hot weather pasta.

Recipe continued following page

Tofu and Pea Pods

½   pound pea pods, trimmed
8   ounces firm tofu, cut into cubes
2   tablespoons water
2   tablespoons shoyu
2   green onions, chopped

In steamer placed over rapidly boiling water, steam peapods until crisp-tender.

Meanwhile, in heavy saucepan over low heat, simmer tofu in water and shoyu 3 minutes.

LEGUMES

Refried Beans

1   cup dried pinto OR kidney beans, presoaked and drained
3   cups water
1   strip kombu
2   bay leaves
    Olive oil
1   large yellow onion, chopped
2   coves garlic, crushed
1   tablespoon shoyu
1   teaspoon prepared yellow mustard
1   teaspoon cumin
½   teaspoon dried oregano
½   teaspoon sea salt, or as desired
1   pinch cayenne pepper
    Chopped green onions (optional)

In pressure cooker, bring beans, water, kombu, and bay leaves to pressure over high heat; reduce heat to low and cook 45 minutes. Drain beans; discard kombu and bay leaves (reserve broth, if desired, for another use). Mash beans with fork in large bowl.

Lightly coat the bottom of large skillet with oil; place over high heat. Sauté yellow onion and garlic 4 minutes or until translucent; reduce heat to low. Stir in shoyu, mustard, cumin, oregano, salt, and cayenne. Stir in mashed beans; cook 5 minutes or until heated through, stirring often. Serve garnished with green onions, if desired.

Black Bean and Corn Salad

    Kernels cut from 2 ears fresh corn
2   cups cooked black beans
1   stalk celery, diced
¼   cup chopped red onion
¼   cup olive oil
3   tablespoons brown rice vinegar
2   tablespoons chopped fresh oregano, OR ½ teaspoon
    dried oregano
1½ teaspoons prepared yellow mustard

1   pinch sea salt, or to taste
1   pinch black pepper
1   tablespoon chopped fresh cilantro

in steamer placed over boiling water, steam corn 3 minutes or until crisp-tender. In large serving bowl, combine corn, beans, celery, and onion.

In small bowl, whisk together oil, vinegar, oregano, mustard, salt, and pepper; pour over corn mixture. Toss lightly; garnish with cilantro.

Chickpea Salad

1   cup dried chickpeas, presoaked and drained
5   cups water
1   strip kombu
1   bay leaf
1   pinch sea salt, or to taste
4   red radishes, sliced
4   green onions, chopped
2   Kirby cucumbers, peeled, seeded, and chopped
⅓   cup sliced black olives, about 12 olives (optional)
3   tablespoons umesu (umeboshi "vinegar")
2   tablespoons olive oil

In pressure cooker, bring chickpeas, water, kombu, bay leaf, and salt to pressure over high heat; reduce heat to low and cook 60 minutes. Drain chickpeas; discard kombu and bay leaf (reserve broth for another use, if desired). Cool chickpeas to room temperature.

In large bowl, combine chickpeas, radishes, green onions, cucumbers, and olives (if desired). In small bowl, whisk together umesu and oil; pour over chickpea mixture. Toss lightly; serve mounded on steamed kale leaves and lettuce, if desired.

Black-Eyed Peas and Rice

1   large onion, minced
    Olive oil
1   clove garlic, crushed
1   pinch sea salt, or to taste

recipe continued folllowing page

2   cups cooked black-eyed peas
2   cups cooked long grain brown rice
2   tablespoons chopped fresh basil or ½ teaspoon
    dried basil
¼   teaspoon dried sage
    Chopped fresh parsley

Lightly coat the bottom of large skillet with oil; place over high heat. Sauté onion and garlic 5 minutes or until translucent; sprinkle with salt. Reduce heat to low; stir in peas, rice, basil, and sage. Cover; cook 10 minutes. If necessary, add a few drops of water to thin to desired consistency. Garnish with parsley; serve hot.

Bean Salad

    Olive Oil Vinaigrette (recipe follows)
1   large yellow onion, minced
    Olive oil
1   strip kombee
1   clove garlic, crushed
1   cup dried mixed beans (such as pinto, kidney, and navy)
    presoaked and drained
3   cups water
4   green onions, chopped
¼   cup sliced red radishes
    Chopped fresh cilantro (optional)

Prepare Olive Oil Vinaigrette; set aside.

Lightly coat the bottom of large soup pot with oil; place over high heat. Sauté onion and garlic 5 minutes or until translucent. Add beans and water; bring to a boil. Cover and reduce heat to low. Cook 1 hour or until tender, adding more water if necessary. Drain beans; let cool to room temperature (reserve stock for another use, if desired).

In large serving bowl, combine beans with green onions and radishes. Pour vinaigrette over; add salt and toss lightly. Garnish with cilantro, if desired.

Olive Oil Vinaigrette

3   tablespoons olive oil
2   tablespoons brown rice vinegar
2   tablespoons fresh lemon juice
½   teaspoon mustard powder
1   pinch sea salt, or to taste

Combine all ingredients in jar with tight-fitting lid; shake vigorously.

Black Beans with Hiziki

3   cups water
1   cup dried black beans, rinsed and drained
½   cup dried hiziki, rinsed and drained
1   strip kombu
¼   teaspoon EACH: dried oregano, basil, and savory
1   clove garlic, crushed (optional)
3   tablespoons shoyu
3   tablespoons chopped green onion

Bring water to a boil in large soup pot over high heat. Add beans; cover and return to a boil. Remove from heat; let stand 1 hour. Place over medium heat and simmer 1½ hours. Stir in hiziki, kombu, oregano, basil, savory, and garlic. Simmer 10 minutes or until all liquid is absorbed. Remove kombu; stir in shoyu and green onion. Serve hot.

Lentil Pâté

    Pastry for double-crust 9-inch pie
2   cups dried lentils, rinsed and drained
4   cups water
2   tablespoons canola oil (optional)
2   cups finely chopped onions (about 2 large)
3   cloves garlic, crushed
1   teaspoon sea salt

recipe continued following page

½   teaspoon dried oregano
¼   teaspoon dried basil
1   teaspoon prepared dijon mustard
2   tablespoons dried bread crumbs
1   tablespoon miso
1   tablespoon boiling water

Preheat oven to 375°F. Lightly oil 9 x 4-inch loaf pan; line bottom and sides with half of pie pastry. Set aside.

In large soup pot, bring lentils and water to a boil over high heat; cover and reduce heat to low. Simmer 20 minutes until lentils are tender and water is absorbed.

Coat heated bottom of large skillet with oil; place over high heat. Sauté onion and garlic 4 minutes or until translucent; sprinkle with salt. Stir in oregano and basil; reduce heat to low. Stir in cooked lentils, mustard, and bread crumbs; cook 3 minutes. Dissolve miso in boiling water; stir into lentil mixture. Remove from heat.

Pour lentil mixture into pastry-lined pan; top with remaining pie pastry. Fold edge over; pinch to seal. Pierce top with fork to allow steam to escape. Bake 45 minutes; cover edge with foil to prevent overbrowning, if necessary. Let stand 15 minutes to cool; carefully remove from pan. Slice and serve with dijon mustard, if desired.

Variation: Pâté can be prepared without pie crust in lightly oiled loaf pan. Slice and serve in pita pockets as a sandwich.

Red Lentil Salad

Red Lentil Vinaigrette (recipe follows)
2   cups water
1   cup red lentils, rinsed and drained
1   strip kombu
1   clove garlic, minced
2   green onions, minced

Prepare Red Lemon Vinaigrette; set aside

Bring water and lentils to a boil in large soup pot over high heat; reduce heat to low. Add kombu and garlic; cover and simmer 30 minutes. Drain off any excess water; cool to room temperature. Remove kombu. In large serving bowl, toss with green onions and vinaigrette. Serve warm or chilled.

RED LENTIL VINAIGRETTE

6   tablespoons olive oil
2   tablespoons fresh lemon juice
1   tablespoon brown rice vinegar
¼   teaspoon tumeric
1   pinch sea salt, or to taste
1   pinch pepper, or to taste
2   green onions, chopped fine

Combine all ingredients in jar with tight-fitting lid; shake vigorously.

Note: Tumeric gives the "orange" appearance to the vinaigrette.

Lentil-Stuffed Cabbage Rolls

2   cups water
½   cup dried lentils, rinsed and drained
1   bay leaf
½   strip kombu
    Olive oil
6   green onions, thinly sliced
3   cloves garlic, minced
1½ cups cooked long grain brown rice
½   cup chopped fresh parsley
2   tablespoons fresh lemon juice
1   teaspoon dried oregano
1   pinch sea salt, or to taste
1   pinch pepper, or to taste
10 napa leaves, cut ¼ inch from base, and steamed until
    pliable
2   cups Basic Vegetable Stock (recipe page 60) OR
    water

recipe continued following page

Place rinsed lentils, kombu, and bay leaf in a pot. Bring to a boil over high heat; reduce heat to low. Cover and simmer 30 minutes. Drain off any excess water; remove kombu and bay leaf.

Coat the bottom of large skillet with oil; place over high heat. Sauté green onions and garlic 4 minutes; reduce heat to low. Stir in cooked lentils, rice, parsley, lemon juice, oregano, salt, and pepper; mix thoroughly. Remove from heat.

Place 1 napa leaf on clean work surface; spoon about 3 tablespoons lentil mixture in center of leaf near bottom. Roll bottom of leaf over filling; turn sides of leaf over, egg-roll style, and roll leaf up to top. Secure with toothpick, if desired, and place seam side-down in large skillet. Repeat with remaining leaves and filling. Pour vegetable stock over and around rolls; place over low heat. Bring to a boil; cover and simmer 10 minutes. Remove from heat; let stand, covered, 10 minutes before serving.

Nutty Lentil Salad

3   cups water
1   cup red lentils, rinsed and drained
1   large yellow onion, minced
1   strip kombu
1   bay leaf
1   clove garlic, minced
¼   teaspoon cumin
6   tablespoons olive oil
3   tablespoons fresh lemon juice
1   teaspoon sea salt
4   green onions, minced
1   stalk celery, chopped
½   cup chopped walnuts (optional)

Bring water to a boil in large soup pot over high heat. Stir in lentils, yellow onion, kombu, bay leaf, garlic and cumin; cover and reduce heat to low. Simmer 30 minutes or until lentils are tender. Drain off any excess liquid; remove kombu and bay leaf. Let cool to room temperature; place in large serving bowl.

In small bowl, whisk together olive oil, lemon juice, and salt; pour over lentil mixture. Add green onions and walnuts; toss lightly. Serve warm or chilled.

Variation: Cilantro-Lentil Salad. Substitute ¼ cup chopped fresh cilantro for the walnuts.

Kidney Beans with Lime Dressing

Lime-Almond Dressing (recipe follows)
Olive oil
1   large yellow onion, chopped
1   clove garlic, minced
1   teaspoon cumin
¼   teaspoon sea salt
2   cups cooked kidney beans
2   tablespoons chopped green onion
1   tablespoon chopped fresh cilantro (optional)

Prepare Lime-Almond Dressing; set aside.

Lightly coat heated bottom of large skillet with oil; place over high heat. Sauté yellow onion and garlic 4 minutes or until translucent; reduce heat to low. Stir in cumin and salt; sauté 2 minutes. Stir in beans; remove from heat. Allow to cool to room temperature; mix with green onion in large serving bowl. Toss with dressing and cilantro (if desired). Adjust the seasoning and purée. Cool and serve as a spread or leave the beans whole, mix with dressing and serve in folded corn tortillas.

LIME DRESSING

3   tablespoons water
2   tablespoons shoyu
1½ tablespoons fresh lime juice
1   tablespoon almond butter
½   teaspoon prepared yellow mustard

Combine all ingredients in blender or food processor; purée until smooth.

White Bean Salad

2   cups cooked white beans (such as Great Northern or cannaline)
1   tomato, seeded and chopped
3   tablespoons chopped red onion
2   tablespoons chopped fresh rosemary or ½ teaspoon dry rosemary
2   tablespoons olive oil
2   tablespoons red wine or balsamic vinegar
½ - 1 teaspoon sea salt
¼   teaspoon dried basil
1   pinch black pepper, or to taste

In large serving bowl, combine beans, tomato, red onion, and rosemary. In small bowl, whisk together oil, vinegar, salt, basil, and pepper; pour over bean mixture. Toss lightly; serve warm or chilled.

Bean and Elbow Macaroni Salad

3-4 cups cooked kidney or pinto beans
1½ cups cooked green beans
10 ounces dried or soy wheat macaroni, cooked and drained
2-3 green onions, finely chopped
½   red bell pepper, sliced
½   cup chopped celery
Vinagrette or Tofu Salad Dressing (recipes page 154)

In a large bowl, combine beans, vegetables, and pasta. Toss gently with dressing of your choice. Serve in lettuce cups.

TOFU & TEMPEH

Baked Tofu Cutlets

1   pound firm tofu, drained
²/₃ cup water
¹/₃ cup shoyu
1   clove garlic, minced
1   teaspoon grated fresh ginger root
6   carrot flowers, for garnish
2   green onions, sliced lengthwise and then cut into 3-inch
    strips, for garnish

Preheat oven to 350°F.

Slice tofu block in half across the width. Cut each half into thirds to make 6 cutlets; place in glass baking dish.

In small bowl, whisk together water, shoyu, garlic, and ginger; pour over tofu. Cover with foil; bake 20 minutes. With metal spatula, carefully remove tofu cutlets to a serving platter. Decorate each cutlet with a carrot flower and a green strip as a stem.

Tofu Fettucini

3   tablespoons shoyu
1   tablespoon brown rice vinegar
¾   teaspoon dried basil
½   teaspoon dried oregano
1   pound firm tofu, drained
    Olive oil
1   pound broccoli florets
    Sea salt
1   pound mushrooms, sliced
1   medium onion, finely chopped
3   cloves garlic, minced
1   pound dried fettucini noodles, cooked and drained

Combine shoyu, vinegar, basil, and oregano. Crumble tofu into shoyu mixture; set aside.

Lightly coat the bottom of large skillet with oil; place over medium heat. Sauté broccoli with a pinch of salt 5 to 7 minutes or until crisp tender;

remove from skillet. Lightly recoat bottom of skillet with oil; sauté mushrooms with a pinch of sea salt over medium heat 5 to 7 minutes or until tender; remove from skillet. Recoat bottom of skillet with oil; sauté onion and garlic with a pinch of salt over medium heat 4 minutes or until translucent. Stir in tofu mixture, cooked broccoli, and mushrooms; cook 3 minutes. Toss with noodles in large serving bowl. Serve immediately.

Tofu Egg-Foo Young

Kuzu Sauce (recipe follows)
½ cup fresh bean sprouts, rinsed and drained
4 dried shiitake mushrooms, soaked and drained according to package directions, knobby stems removed, caps sliced
1 egg, lightly beaten (or egg substitute)
8 ounces firm tofu, drained, crumbled
½ cup chopped green onions
2 tablespoons shoyu
1 pinch sea salt
Canola oil

Prepare Kuzu Sauce; keep warm.

In large bowl, combine all ingredients except oil; mix well. Lightly coat the bottom of large skillet with oil; place over medium heat. Using a ¼-cup measure, scoop batter into skillet to form 3 to 4 patties. Cook until golden, about 3 minutes. Carefully flip patties with metal spatula; cook other side 2 to 3 minutes until golden; remove to paper towel-lined platter. Keep warm. Repeat with remaining batter. Serve with warm Kuzu Sauce.

KUZU SAUCE

1 tablespoon kuzu
1 cup Basic Vegetable Stock (recipe page 60) OR water
1 tablespoon shoyu
1 teaspoon grated fresh ginger root
¼ teaspoon garlic powder

Recipe continued following page

Dissolve kuzu in cool vegetable stock or water in small saucepan; stir in shoyu. Bring to a boil over high heat; reduce heat to low. Add the ginger and garlic; simmer 3 minutes. Remove from heat. Stir the kuzu mixture as it thickens to prevent clumping.

Tofu-Bulgur Burger

1   large mushroom, minced
    Canola oil
1   red bell pepper, cored, seeded, and finely chopped
½   cup bulgur, rinsed and drained
½   cup boiling water
1   pound firm tofu, drained, crumbled
1   egg, lightly beaten OR egg replacer
3   tablespoons shoyu
3   tablespoons fresh grated yellow onion
3   tablespoons chopped green onion
¼   teaspoon dried basil

Lightly coat the bottom of large skillet with oil; place over high heat. Sauté mushroom 1 minute; stir in bell pepper and reduce heat to medium. Sauté 3 minutes or until softened. Stir in bulgur; pour boiling water over. Cover; let simmer 1 minute. Remove from heat; let stand, covered, 30 minutes.

Stir in tofu, egg or egg replacer, shoyu, yellow onion, green onion, and basil; mix well. Form mixture into ½-inch patties; place patties on waxed paper.

Lightly coat heated bottom of large skillet with oil; place over medium heat. Fry patties, 3 to 4 at a time, 3 minutes on each side or until golden. Repeat with remaining patties. Serve warm with Horseradish Sauce (recipe page 156), if desired.

Scrambled Tofu

1   medium onion, finely chopped
    Canola oil
8   ounces firm tofu, drained, crumbled
1   pinch sea salt, or to taste

Shoyu, to taste
¼ teaspoon garlic powder
⅛ teaspoon tumeric
Chopped fresh parsley

Lightly coat the bottom of large skillet with oil; place over high heat. Sauté onion 4 minutes or until translucent; reduce heat to medium. Stir in tofu and salt; sauté 4 minutes. Add a few drops shoyu to taste. Stir in garlic and tumeric; remove from heat. Serve hot garnished with parsley.

Stuffed Age Pouches

Ginger-Kuzu Sauce (recipe follows on page 126)
toasted sesame oil
1 clove garlic, crushed
6 fresh shiitake mushrooms, sliced
3 cups shredded napa cabbage
8 ounces dried somen, broken into approximate thirds, cooked, and drained
6 green onions, finely chopped
1 tablespoon shoyu
12 small age pouches*

Prepare Ginger-Kuzu Sauce; set aside.

Preheat oven to 350ºF. Lightly oil 9 x 12-inch glass baking dish; set aside.

Lightly coat the bottom of large skillet with toasted sesame oil; place over high heat. Sauté garlic 1 minute; reduce heat to low. Stir in mushrooms, cabbage, somen, and green onions; sauté 4 minutes. Stir in shoyu and sesame oil; remove from heat.

Carefully slit open one side of an age pouch, opening gradually to avoid tearing. Stuff with some of noodle mixture; secure end with toothpick and place in prepared pan. Repeat with remaining pouches and noodle mixture. Spoon Ginger-Kuzu Sauce over pouches; cover with foil. Bake 20 minutes; serve immediately.

*Age pouches are available in oriental markets and some supermarkets.

GINGER-KUZU SAUCE

1   heaping tablespoon kuzu
1   cup cool water
1   tablespoon shoyu
1   teaspoon grated fresh ginger root

In medium saucepan, dissolve kuzu in water; stir in shoyu. Bring to a boil over medium heat, stirring often to prevent lumps from forming. Reduce heat to low; stir in ginger and simmer 1 minute. Remove from heat.

Hot Tempeh Slices

16   ounces tempeh
2   cups water
½   cup shoyu
1   tablespoon grated fresh ginger root
2   cloves garlic, minced

Slice tempeh block in half lengthwise; cut 8 slices horizontally to make 16 slices. In large saucepan, bring water, shoyu, ginger, and garlic to a boil; reduce heat to low. Add tempeh slices; simmer 20 minutes. Remove tempeh with a slotted metal spoon; reserve liquid for another seasoning use, if desired.

Serve hot tempeh surrounded by steamed greens, with cooked vegetables and Kuzu Sauce (recipe page 123), or in a pita pocket with hot mustard and lettuce.

Tempeh Pâté

8   ounces tempeh
2   cups water
¼   cup shoyu
1   clove garlic, minced
1½ tablespoons grated fresh ginger root
2   green onions, chopped

2 tablespoons finely chopped dill pickle
1 stalk celery, chopped
1 tablespoon Tofu Mayonnaise (recipe page 151)
1 tablespoon umesu (umeboshi "vinegar")
1 teaspoon prepared mustard (optional)

In large saucepan over medium heat, bring tempeh, water, shoyu, garlic, and ginger to a boil; reduce heat to low. Simmer 20 minutes; drain. Purée cooked tempeh in blender or food processor; stir in remaining ingredients. Serve warm or chilled on a bed of blanched kale with toasted pita slices.

Tempeh Salad

8 ounces tempeh, cut into ½-inch cubes
Olive oil
¼ cup Tofu Mayonnaise (recipe page 151)
2 green onions, minced
1 dill pickle, finely chopped
1 teaspoon prepared white horseradish
1 pinch sea salt
1 pinch pepper

Lightly coat heated bottom of large skillet with oil; place over medium heat. Stir-fry tempeh cubes until golden and crisp; remove from skillet to paper towel-lined platter.

In large bowl, combine tempeh cubes with remaining ingredients; mix well. Serve warm with couscous or chilled on a bed of steamed kale leaves or romaine lettuce.

SEITAN & FU

Basic Seitan

SEITAN
5   pounds whole-wheat flour
8   cups water

SEASONING MIX
½ - ¼ cup shoyu, or as desired
8   cloves garlic
2   tablespoons ginger juice or 4 tablespoons grated ginger root
½   teaspoon dried rosemary (optional)
2   bay leaves
1-2 tablespoons oil (optional)

Place flour in a large bowl; gradually stir in water. Turn dough out onto lightly floured surface; knead for 5 to 8 minutes. Return dough to bowl; cover with lukewarm water and allow to rest for 20 minutes.

Drain off starchy liquid; reserve for later use as a thickener in sauces, if desired. Knead dough in bowl and rinse under alternating warm and cool water, until little bran or starch remains.

Drop balls of gluten dough into water in a large pot. Bring to a boil over high heat. When gluten balls float to the surface, reduce heat to low. Stir in Seasoning Mix. Cover; reduce heat to low and simmer 1 hour.

Cooked seitan can be refrigerated in a large jar packed with simmering broth and later sliced for sandwiches, sautéed in cutlets, and many other uses.

Seitan Kebabs

1   tablespoon olive oil (optional)
1   tablespoon shoyu
2   cloves garlic, crushed
½   teaspoon EACH: dried basil and oregano
2   large carrots, roll-cut on a diagonal, steamed until crisp-tender
12 mushrooms

recipe continued following page

2   onions, cut into wedges
1   head of broccoli, cut into large florets

Preheat grill or broiler.

Combine oil, shoyu, garlic, basil, and oregano in a large non-metallic bowl. Stir in carrots, mushrooms, seitan, onion wedges, and broccoli until evenly coated. Let stand 10 minutes. Drain; reserve marinade.

Alternately thread vegetables and seitan onto 6 skewers. Grill or broil for 4 to 5 minutes, brushing occasionally with reserved marinade.

Seitan Stroganoff

1   large onion, chopped
    Canola or olive oil
2   cloves garlic, crushed
1   teaspoon sea salt
6   ounces silken tofu, puréed
3 - 4 tablespoons sake (optional)
2   tablespoons shoyu
10- 12 mushrooms, sliced
2 - 3 cups seitan, cut into ¼-inch strips
¼   teaspoon dried basil
2   tablespoons chopped fresh parsley

Lightly coat the bottom of large skillet with oil; place over high heat. Sauté onion 3 to 4 minutes or until translucent. Stir in garlic; sprinkle with

salt. Stir in tofu; cook 2 to 3 minutes. Stir in sake and shoyu until well blended. Remove from heat.

Lightly coat the bottom of another large skillet with oil; place over high heat. Sauté mushrooms 3 to 4 minutes until they just begin to brown. Stir in seitan. Cook, covered, over low heat until mushrooms are tender. Stir in basil. Pour tofu mixture over seitan-mushroom mixture; simmer 3 to 4 minutes. Serve hot over soba or rice; garnish with parsley.

Seitan Pot Pie

2   cups seitan, cut into ¼-inch strips
    Canola or olive oil
2   cloves garlic, crushed
2   large potatoes, peeled and cut into ½-inch cubes
1   large carrot, cut into matchsticks
½   cup fresh green peas
1   pinch sea salt
1   pinch dried rosemary
1   cup Basic Brown Sauce (recipe page 158)
    Pastry for double-crust pie (recipe page 185)

Lightly coat the bottom of large skillet with oil; place over high heat. Sauté seitan with garlic 3 to 4 minutes. Sprinkle with salt and rosemary; sauté 1 minute. Remove seitan mixture with slotted spoon; place in large bowl. Reheat the skillet and either "water sauté" the carrot sticks or lightly oil the skillet to sauté them. Repeat with the potato cubes. Combine all, add peas, and gently mix with brown suace.

Preheat oven to 350ºF. Lightly oil 8-inch deep-dish pie plate.

Roll out one-half of pastry dough; place pastry in bottom of prepared pie plate. Fill with seitan-vegetable mixture. Roll out second half of pastry dough; place over seitan-vegetable mixture. Fold edges over; flute. Pierce top with fork to allow steam to escape. Bake 30 to 35 minutes until golden; remove to wire rack. Let stand 5 minutes before cutting and serving.

Seitan-Vegetable Medley

2   large carrots, roll-cut on a diagonal
    Olive oil
1   teaspoon grated fresh ginger root
8   ounces seitan, sliced into ¼-inch strips
1   large onion, cut into 6 wedges
½   bunch broccoli, cut into florets
½   cauliflower, cut into florets
1   large baking potato, peeled and sliced into ovals
    Kuzu Sauce (recipe page 123)

recipe continued following page

Lightly coat the bottom of large skillet with oil or warm a few tablespoons of water; place over high heat. Sauté carrots and ginger for 1 to 2 minutes; reduce heat to low. Sprinkle with water; cover and steam 5 minutes or until tender. Remove carrots with a slotted spoon; arrange in a row on a large serving platter. Recoat skillet with oil; sauté seitan 5 minutes until golden. Remove with slotted spoon and place next to carrots on serving platter. Repeat with broccoli, cauliflower, and potato; arrange in separate rows on serving platter. Pour Kuzu Sauce over seitan and vegetables; serve immediately.

Variation: Sliced burdock root, shiitake mushrooms, cabbage wedges, and chopped turnips may be substituted for any of the vegetables.

Seitan Fajitas

1	medium onion, sliced into rings
	Olive oil
1	red bell pepper, cored, seeded and sliced
8	ounces seitan, sliced into ¼-inch strips
1	clove garlic, crushed
¼	teaspoon cumin
⅛	teaspoon oregano
⅛	teaspoon sea salt
1	teaspoon olive oil
1	pinch of black pepper
1	tablespoon fresh lime juice
2	tablespoons fresh minced cilantro
6	whole-wheat tortillas, warmed
	Guacamole

Lightly coat the bottom of large skillet with oil; place over high heat. Sauté onion with bell pepper 3 to 4 minutes or until crisp-tender. Remove from skillet to large non-metallic bowl. Recoat skillet with oil; place over medium heat. Sauté seitan strips, turning often to avoid burning. Add seitan to onion-bell pepper mixture. Whisk together 1 teaspoon olive oil, garlic, cumin, oregano, salt, black pepper, and lime juice. Pour over seitan-vegetable mixture; toss lightly to coat. Reheat vegetables in skillet over high heat 1 minute; stir in cilantro.

Spoon evenly into warmed tortillas; roll up tortillas. Serve with guacamole, if desired.

Fu "Stew"

1   large onion, sliced into rings
    Olive oil or canola oil
1   pinch sea salt
1   package shonai or syonai fu, soaked according to
    package directions
2   tablespoons shoyu
½   pound mushrooms, sliced
½   cup fresh green peas
¼   teaspoon dried thyme
¼   teaspoon dried basil

Lightly coat the bottom of skillet with oil; place over high heat. Sauté onion 3 to 4 minutes or until translucent. Sprinkle with salt; cover. Reduce heat to low and cook for 4 to 5 minutes or until onion is soft. Gently press water out of fu; slice horizontally into ¼-inch strips. Stir fu and shoyu into skillet with onion.

Meanwhile, lightly coat heated bottom of another large skillet with oil; place over high heat. Sauté mushrooms 3 to 4 minutes or until lightly browned. Add to fu-vegetable mixture. Cover and cook 10 to 15 minutes over low heat, stirring occasionally. Stir in peas, thyme, and basil; cook 2 minutes. Serve immediately.

Variation: Fu Stew can be stuffed into steamed butternut squash halves, topped with a spoonful of Miso-Almond Butter Sauce (recipe page 156), and baked in 350°F oven 10 to 12 minutes.

VEGETABLES

Asparagus with Chinese Black Bean Sauce

2 pounds asparagus spears, trimmed
2 cloves garlic
2 tablespoons fermented oriental black beans, soaked, drained, and chopped
1 cup Basic Vegetable Stock (recipe page 60)
1 tablespoon kuzu, dissolved in 1 tablespoon water
1 tablespoon plus 1 teaspoon sesame oil, divided
1 tablespoon shoyu
1 tablespoon sake
1 teaspoon brown rice syrup

Steam asparagus over boiling water 5 minutes or until crisp-tender; remove from heat.

Mash together black beans and garlic with fork in medium bowl until smooth; whisk in kuzu mixture, 1 teaspoon sesame oil, shoyu, sake, and rice syrup.

Heat remaining 1 tablespoon sesame oil in large skillet over low heat; stir in asparagus. Stir-fry 1 minute; stir in black bean mixture. Cook 2 minutes or until sauce boils and thickens. Sprinkle with sesame seeds; serve with steamed rice or other grains.

Baked Greens

1½ pounds fresh greens (such as kale or watercress), rinsed, trimmed
1 teaspoon olive oil or 2 tablespoons vegtable stock (recipe on page 60)
1 clove garlic, crushed
1 teaspoon grated fresh ginger root
½ teaspoon sea salt
¼ - ½ teaspoon curry powder
⅛ teaspoon ground nutmeg
2 tablespoons dry roasted sliced almonds (optional)

Preheat oven to 350°F. Lightly oil 9 x 12-inch glass baking dish; set aside.

Steam greens over boiling water 5 minutes or until tender but still bright green; drain.

Combine greens with oil, garlic, ginger, salt, curry powder, and nutmeg in food processor or blender; pureé until smooth. Spread mixture evenly in prepared baking dish; top with almonds (if desired). Bake 25 minutes; serve hot.

Shredded Brussel Sprouts

½   pound Brussel sprouts, rinsed, trimmed
     Olive oil
¼   teaspoon sea salt
1   tablespoon fresh lime juice or balsamic vinegar
¼   teaspoon garlic powder
1   pinch black pepper
1   teaspoon water

Shred Brussels sprouts by thinly slicing lengthwise into small pieces. Lightly coat the bottom of skillet with oil; place over medium heat. Sauté Brussels sprouts 3 minutes; sprinkle with salt. Stir in lime juice, garlic powder, and pepper; sauté 2 minutes. Sprinkle with water; cover and steam 2 minutes. Serve hot.

Lemony Watercress Pinwheels

     Water
1   pinch sea salt
4   large outer leaves napa cabbage, rinsed
2   bunches watercress, rinsed
1   tablespoon EACH: brown rice vinegar, shoyu, fresh lemon juice, mirin

Bring about 2 inches of water to a rolling boil with sea salt in large soup pot over high heat. Add cabbage; boil 2 minutes or until bright-colored and pliable. Remove cabbage with slotted spoon; rinse with cool water and drain.

Return water to a rolling boil. Blanch watercress in batches 1 to 2 minutes or until bright green; rinse with cool water and drain.

Whisk together vinegar, shoyu, lemon juice, and mirin in small non-metallic bowl; set aside.

Place 1 cabbage leaf on a bamboo mat; place ¼ of watercress down center. Sprinkle with some of vinegar mixture. Using bamboo mat, roll into a compact cylinder. Slice into 1-inch pieces. Repeat with remaining napa, watercress, and vinegar mixture. Serve with additional shoyu for dipping.

Cabbage-Tempeh Sauté

½	pound tempeh, thinly sliced
	Olive oil
1	pinch sea salt
1	pound napa cabbage, chopped
1	medium onion, minced
1	clove garlic, minced
¼	cup dry white wine or 3 tablespoons sake
1	bay leaf
¼	teaspoon thyme
1	medium carrot, grated

Lightly coat the bottom of large skillet with oil; place over high heat. Sauté tempeh 2 minutes; sprinkle with salt and reduce heat to low. Sauté 5 minutes until crisp and golden; remove to paper towel-lined platter.

Recoat skillet with oil; place over high heat. Sauté cabbage and onion 2 minutes; reduce heat to low. Stir in garlic, wine, bay leaf, and thyme. Cover and simmer 8 minutes. Stir in carrot and top with sautéed tempeh; simmer 1 minute. Remove bay leaf; serve immediately.

Cauliflower Sauté

1	head cauliflower, cut into florets
	Olive oil
1	clove garlic, minced
6	green onions, minced
1	red bell pepper, cored, seeded, and sliced
1	tablespoon fresh lemon juice
¼	teaspoon sea salt

recipe continued following page

Blanch cauliflower in boiling water 1 minute; drain and rinse with cool water. Drain again.

Lightly coat the bottom of large skillet with oil; place over high heat. Sauté garlic 1 minute; reduce heat to low. Add green onions; sauté 3 minutes. Stir in bell pepper and cauliflower; sauté 3 minutes. Sprinkle with lemon juice and salt; sauté 3 minutes or until cauliflower is tender. Serve immediately.

Note: This basic preparation can be used for broccoli, green beans, and other fibrous vegetables.

Blanched Vegetable Salad

1   leek, thoroughly rinsed and sliced on a diagonal
1   head cauliflower, cut into florets
1   large carrot, cut into matchsticks
¼   cup sliced black olives (optional)
3   tablespoons umesu (umeboshi "vinegar")
2   tablespoons olive oil
    Zest from 1 orange (outermost part of peel)

Bring about 2 inches of water to a boil in a large soup pot. Blanch leeks 1 minute or until bright green; remove with slotted spoon to colander. Rinse with cool water and drain. Separate leaves into a large serving bowl.

Blanch cauliflower and carrots in same soup pot 2 minutes; drain in colander. Rinse with cool water and drain. Combine with leeks; stir in black olives (if desired).

In small bowl, whisk together umeboshi, oil, and orange zest; pour over leek-vegetable mixture. Toss to coat; serve warm or chilled.

Savory Onion Tart

1   prepared pie pastry for single-crust pie (recipe page 185)
1   tablespoon toasted oat bran flakes or dry bread crumbs
    Olive oil
2   large yellow onions, thinly sliced

2   green onions, thinly sliced
¼   cup dried sun-dried tomatoes, soaked according to
    package directions, drained, chopped
¼   teaspoon sea salt, or to taste
½   teaspoon dried basil
¼   cup sliced black olives

Place pie pastry in tart pan with removable bottom; flute edges or press with tines of fork. Sprinkle bran flakes over pastry; set aside.

Lightly coat the bottom of large skillet with oil; place over high heat. Sauté yellow onions 3 minutes; stir in green onions and reduce heat to low. Cover and cook 30 minutes until tender and caramel-colored. Stir in sun-dried tomatoes; cook 2 minutes. Stir in salt and basil; spoon into prepared tart shell. Preheat oven to 425°F. Top with black olives; cook 20 minutes or until crust is golden and flaky.

Kale-Stuffed Onions

6   medium yellow onions
    Olive oil
2   cloves garlic, minced
¼   teaspoon sea salt
1   pound kale, rinsed, stems removed, and chopped
⅓   cup silken tofu, drained
2   tablespoons sliced pine nuts or blanched almonds
1   teaspoon orange zest (outermost part of peel)
2   tablespoons fresh bread crumbs

Preheat oven to 350°F. Lightly oil 9 x 12-inch baking dish.

Slice off a small piece from root end of onions to make bottoms level. Peel off papery outer skin. Scoop out inside flesh with melon ball or spoon to make a ½-inch shell; mince scooped-out onion flesh and set aside.

Steam onion shells over boiling water 12 minutes or until tender; drain.

Meanwhile, lightly coat the bottom of large skillet with oil; place over high heat. Sauté reserved minced onion with garlic 4 minutes of until translucent; sprinkle with salt and reduce heat to low. Stir in kale; cover and steam 3 minutes. Remove from heat; mix in tofu, pine nuts, and orange zest until

recipe continued following page

well combined. Spoon onion-tofu mixture into onion shells; place in prepared baking dish. Sprinkle tops with bread crumbs. Bake 20 minutes or until topping is golden brown.

Tempeh-Stuffed Onions

6   medium yellow onions
    Olive oil
2   cloves garlic, minced
6   ounces tempeh, cut into cubes
    Water
2   cups minced mushrooms
2   tablespoons shoyu
1   tablespoon fresh grated ginger root
½   cup cooked brown rice
¼   teaspoon thyme
1   pinch sea salt

Preheat oven to 350°F. Lightly oil 9 x 12-inch baking dish.

Slice off a small piece from root end of onions to make bottoms level. Peel off papery outer skin. Scoop out inside flesh with melon ball or spoon to make a ½-inch shell; mince scooped-out onion flesh and set aside.

Steam onion shells over boiling water 12 minutes or until tender; drain.

Meanwhile, lightly coat the bottom of large skillet with oil; place over high heat. Sauté reserved minced onion with garlic 4 minutes of until translucent; stir in tempeh and reduce heat to low. Sauté 4 minutes until tempeh turns golden; sprinkle with water, if necessary, to prevent sticking. Stir in mushrooms, shoyu, and ginger; cook 4 minutes. Stir in rice, thyme, and sea salt; remove from heat. Spoon tempeh mixture into onion shells; place in prepared baking dish. Bake 10 minutes or until hot. Serve immediately.

Squash with Onions and Almonds

1   butternut squash
    Canola oil (optional)
1   large onions, thinly sliced into rings

¼   teaspoon sea salt
    Water
2   tablespoons sliced almonds

Cut squash in half vertically. Scoop out seeds; reserve seeds for a toasted snack, if desired. Slice squash crosswise into cubes; cut off outer skin, if desired.

Lightly coat heated bottom of large skillet with oil; place over high heat. Sauté onion 4 minutes or until translucent or "sauté" in a small amount of water; stir in squash and reduce heat to low. Sprinkle with salt; cook 1 minute. Add enough water to come halfway up sides of squash (about ¼ cup); cover and simmer 20 minutes or until squash is tender. Drain off any excess water; sprinkle with almonds. Serve hot.

Baked Squash Pureé

1   buttercup or butternut squash
    Water
1   onion, chopped
1   tablespoon sweet white miso
1   tablespoon almond butter
⅛   teaspoon EACH: dried thyme, sea salt, white pepper
1   tablespoon almond slices

Preheat oven to 350°F. Lightly oil 9 x 12-inch baking dish.

Cut squash in half vertically. Scoop out seeds; reserve seeds for a toasted snack, if desired. Place squash halves in prepared baking dish; bake 45 minutes or until tender. Add water, if necessary, to prevent scorching.

Meanwhile, bring ½ cup water to a boil in medium saucepan. Boil onion 8 minutes until tender; drain.

Carefully scoop out squash flesh from skins; combine with onions, miso, almond butter, thyme, salt, and white pepper in food processor or blender. Pureé until smooth. Spoon into lightly oiled baking dish; bake at 350°F for 15 minutes. Garnish with almond slices; serve hot.

Spaghetti Squash with Sesame Sauce

1   large spaghetti squash
1   teaspoon olive oil (optional)
1   tablespoon toasted tahini
2   teaspoons fresh lemon juice
1   clove garlic, crushed
⅛   teaspoon dried basil
1   pinch white pepper (optional)
¼   cup boiling Basic Vegetable Stock (recipe page 60) OR
     water
2   green onions, chopped

Steam the uncut squash over boiling water 30 minutes or until fork-tender.

Meanwhile, whisk together tahini, lemon juice, garlic, basil, and white pepper in medium bowl. Whisk in boiling vegetable stock; set aside.

Carefully cut squash in half lengthwise. Scoop out seeds and pulp; discard. Scrape out "spaghetti" strands of squash with tines of a fork; place in large serving bowl. Pour hot tahini mixture over; toss lightly to coat. Top with green onions.

Vegetables à la Grecque

1   head cauliflower, cut into florets
½   pound green beans, trimmed
1   large carrot, cut into matchsticks
10   large mushrooms, sliced
1   cup cooked chickpeas
¼   cup sliced black olives
1   10" piece of wakame, soaked and drained according to
     package directions, tough stipe removed, and sliced
3   tablespoons olive oil
3   tablespoons orange juice
2   tablespoons brown rice vinegar
2   tablespoons fresh lemon juice
2   tablespoons fresh lime juice
1   tablespoon shoyu

1   clove garlic, minced
½   teaspoon dried oregano
1   pinch sea salt

Blanch cauliflower in boiling water 2 minutes; remove with slotted spoon and drain. Repeat with green beans, carrot, and mushrooms. Combine cooked vegetables with chickpeas (if desired), black olives, and wakame in large serving bowl.

In medium non-metallic bowl, whisk together remaining ingredients; pour over vegetable mixture. Toss lightly to coat; serve warm or chilled.

SALADS

Pressed Cabbage Salad

½ head of cabbage, shredded
½ cup grated carrots
2 green onions, finely chopped
1 teaspoon sea salt
Tofu Salad Dressing (recipe page 154) OR salad dressing
of your choice

Toss together cabbage and carrots in large non-metallic bowl; sprinkle with salt. Press a plate that fits inside of bowl on top of cabbage mixture; weight heavily with canned goods or dried beans. Let stand 1 hour.

Remove weighted plate. Rinse cabbage mixture thoroughly to remove excess salt. Toss with Tofu Salad Dressing; serve chilled.

Variations: Grated daikon, turnip, or other firm root vegetables can be substituted for cabbage and carrots.

Cucumber Cilantro Salad

2 large cucumbers, peeled, seeded, diced
1 teaspoon umersu (umeboshi "vinegar")
½ red bell pepper, cored, seeded, chopped
3 tablespoons chopped fresh cilantro
2½ tablepoons shoyu
2 tablespoons brown rice vinegar
1 tablespoon sesame oil
1 pinch white pepper

Toss cucumbers with umeboshi in large non-metallic bowl. Press a plate that fits inside of bowl on top of cucmuber mixture; weight heavily with vegetable cans or beans. Let stand 1 hour.

Remove wieghted plate; rinse cucumber and drain. Toss with bell pepper and cilantro. Wisk together shoyu, rice vinegar, sesame oil, and white pepper; pour over cucumber mixture. Toss to coat; serve chilled.

Carrot-Daikon Salad

3   large carrots, grated
½   cup grated daikon
2   green onions, minced
½   teaspoon grated fresh ginger root
2   tablespoons unroasted sesame oil or Canola oil
1   tablespoon rice vinegar
¼   teaspoon brown rice syrup
¼   teaspoon sea salt
1   tablespoons toasted sesame seeds

In large serving bowl, toss together carrots, daikon, green onions, and ginger. In small bowl, whisk together sesame oil, vinegar, rice syrup, and salt; pour over carrot mixture. Toss to coat; sprinkle with sesame seeds. Serve warm or chilled.

Sesame-Veggie Salad

    Sesame Dressing (recipe follows next page)
1   bok choy, white portion and green top separated, sliced
1   head cauliflower, cut into florets
6   red radishes, sliced
1   large carrot, cut into matchsticks
1   large cucumber, peeled, seeded, and chopped
1   tablespoon toasted sesame seeds (optional)

Prepeare Sesame Dressing; set aside.

Steam bokchoy, cauliflower, radishes, and carrot until crisp-tender; immediately rinse with cold water to stop cooking process. Toss with cucumber in large serving bowl. Pour dressing over vegetables; toss lightly to coat. Sprinkle with sesame seeds (if desired). Serve warm or chilled.

SESAME DRESSING

2 tablespoons toasted sesame oil
3 tablespoons rice vinegar
2 tablespoons shoyu
½ teaspoon mustard powder

Combine all ingredients in jar with tight-fitting lid; shake vigorously.

Green Beans with Dill Vinaigrette

1 pound fresh green beans, trimmed
½ red onion, thinly sliced into rings
3 tablespoons olive oil
2 tablespoons fresh lemon juice
2 cloves garlic, minced
2 tablespoons chopped fresh dill weed
½ - 1 teaspoon prepared dijon mustard
¼ teaspoon sea salt or umeboshi "vinegar," or to taste

Steam green beans over boiling water 3 minutes until crisp-tender; rinse with cold water to stop the cooking process. Combine with red onion in large serving bowl. In small bowl, whisk together remaining ingredients; pour over green bean mixture. Toss lightly to coat; serve warm or chilled.

Turnips in Raspberry-Lime Vinaigrette

4 turnips, peeled, cut into matchstick pieces
6 red radishes, sliced
2 green onions, cut into 2-inch pieces
3 tablespoons fresh lime juice
1 tablespoon olive oil
1 tablespoon raspberry vinegar
1 teaspoon brown rice syrup
⅛ teaspoon sea salt

Recipe continued on following page

Steam turnips over boiling water 2 minutes; add radishes and green onions. Steam 1 minute; rinse under cold water to stop the cooking process.

Meanwhile, combine lime juice, olive, vinegar, rice syrup, and salt in small saucepan; place over low heat until warm. Toss with turnip mixture in large serving bowl. Serve warm.

Wakame/Jicama Salad

1	large jicama, peeled and sliced in matchsticks
1	12" inch wakame
1	naval orange, peeled and separated into segments
1	small onion, sliced in half moons (optional)
2	tablespoons lime juice
1	small clove garlic, crushed (optional)
2	tablespoons olive oil (optional)
2	teaspoons brown rice or balsamic vinegar
2	teaspoons cilantro, minced
	sea salt, to taste
	pepper, to taste

Bring ¼ inch water to a boil in a skillet with a pinch of sea salt and water "sauté" the sliced onion, covering and cooking until tender. Drain, remove to a bowl with a slotted spoon and cool. Soak the wakame in cool water to 1 to 2 minutes or just until rehydrated. Remove the tough center "stripe" of the wakame and slice the softened fronds into strips approximately $1/8$ inch thick. Combine the lime juice with the remaining ingredients and toss with the jicama, wakame, onion, and orange segments. Serve cool as a refreshing summer salad.

SAUCES, DIPS & DRESSINGS

Shoyu-Ginger Dipping Sauce

3   tablespoons shoyu
3   tablespoons water
½   teaspoon grated fresh ginger root

Combine all ingredients; mix well. Serve with rolled greens for dipping.

Three Flavors Dressing

1   tablespoon shoyu
1   tablespoon brown rice vinegar
1   tablespoon mirin

Combine all ingredients in jar with tight-fitting lid; shake vigorously. Serve as a non-fat dressing for salads.

Variation: Add 1 tablespoon lemon juice to above ingredients to make Ponzu Sauce.

Lime Salad Dressing

    Juice from 1 lime
4   ounces silken tofu, drained OR 4 tablespoons olive oil
1   tablespoon grated onion
1   clove garlic, crushed
1   tablespoon chopped fresh cilantro
½   teaspoon sea salt
⅛   teaspoon cumin

Combine all ingredients in jar with tight-fitting lid; shake vigorously.

Pumpkin Seed Sauce

1   cup roasted pumpkin seed meats
½   cup water
2   tablespoons fresh lemon juice
1   tablespoon white miso
1   tablespoon rice vinegar
2   green onions, finely chopped
    Chopped fresh cilantro (optional)

Place pumpkin seeds, water, lemon juice, miso, and vinegar in blender or food processor; blend until smooth. Stir in green onions and cilantro, if desired. Serve warmed or chilled. Refrigerate leftovers.

Sweet Miso Salad Dressing

4   tablespoons sweet white miso
4   tablespoons fresh lemon juice
3-4 tablespoons water
1   tablespoon grated onion
1   tablespoon canola oil (optional)
½   teaspoon shoyu or tamari, to taste

Purée all ingredients in blender or food processor until smooth.

Tofu Mayonnaise

1   cup silken tofu, drained
1   clove garlic, crushed
1   tablespoon fresh lemon juice
1   teaspoon prepared yellow mustard
1   teaspoon brown rice syrup
¼   teaspoon sea salt

Purée all ingredients in blender or food processor until smooth. Add a few drops of water to thin to desired consistency if necessary.

Lime-Miso-Mustard Dressing

2   tablespoons tahini
2   tablespoons white or rice miso
2   tablespoons fresh lime juice
2   tablespoons olive oil
1   clove garlic, crushed (optional)
4   tablespoons boiling water
1   teaspoon brown rice syrup

In medium saucepan, lightly toast tahini and miso over medium heat 5 minutes, stirring constantly; remove from heat. Whisk in lime juice until well blended. Whisk in remaining ingredients, one at a time, blending thoroughly after each addition. Let cool to room temperature; stir before pouring over salad.

Miso Dressing

4   tablespoons sweet white miso
3   tablespoons olive oil or canola oil
1   tablespoon brown rice vinegar
1   tablespoon fresh lemon juice
1   teaspoon prepared yellow mustard (optional)
1½ teaspoons shoyu
½   cup chopped green onions
2   tablespoons grated or minced yellow onion
3   tablespoons water, as needed

Combine all ingredients in blender or food processor; purée until smooth. Add additional water to thin to desired consistency, if necessary.

Savory Olive Oil Sauce

4   tablespoons olive oil
4   tablespoons brown rice vinegar
3   cloves garlic, crushed
1   tablespoon prepared dijon mustard

1 tablespoon brown rice syrup
¼ cup chopped fresh cilantro
¼ teaspoon sea salt
4 green onions, chopped

Combine all ingredients except green onions is a medium saucepan; simmer over low heat 1 hour. Stir in green onions. Toss with steamed greens or pour over poached fish filets.

Sesame-Citrus Marinade

   Juice from 2 oranges
   Juice from 1 lime
2 cloves garlic, crushed
1 teaspoon grated fresh ginger root
4 tablespoons untoasted sesame oil or Canola oil
4 tablespoons brown rice vinegar
3 tablespoons shoyu
1 pinch sea salt

Whisk together orange juice, lime juice, garlic, and ginger. Whisk in oil, vinegar, shoyu, and salt. Use as a marinade for fish before grilling, or simmer over low heat for a sauce for steamed greens.

Sesame-Umeboshi Dressing

4 tablespoons sesame oil
4 tablespoons umesu (umeboshi "vinegar")
1 clove garlic, crushed
2 tablespoons shoyu
1¼ teaspoons mirin
¼ teaspoon ginger juice

Combine all ingredients in jar with tight-fitting lid; shake vigorously. Refrigerate leftovers.

Tofu Salad Dressing

8   ounces silken tofu, drained
1   tablespoon grated onion
1   tablespoon umesu (umeboshi "vinegar"), or to taste
1   tablespoon water or oil

Parboil tofu in boiling salted water 3 minutes; drain. Cool to room temperature. Blend with remaining ingredients. Additional water may be added to thin to desired consistency.

Green Onion-Kuzu Sauce

1   heaping tablespoon kuzu
1   cup cool water
1   tablespoon shoyu
5   green onions, finely chopped
1   teaspoon toasted sesame oil (optional)

In medium saucepan, dissolve kuzu in water; stir in shoyu. Simmer over medium heat 3 minutes or until clear, stirring constantly to prevent any lumps from forming. Stir in green onions and oil; simmer 30 seconds. Serve over cooked grains.

Variation: For an oil-free sauce, substitute 1 tablespoon grated fresh ginger root for sesame oil.

Note: For a richer flavor, lightly sauté the green onions before adding to sauce.

Simple Vinaigrette

½   cup olive oil or canola oil
1   clove garlic, minced
2   tablespoons brown rice vinegar
1   tablespoon fresh lemon juice (optional)
1   teaspoon prepared mustard

1   teaspoon sea salt
⅛ teaspoon black pepper, or to taste

In large non-metallic bowl whisk together oil and garlic; whisk in remaining ingredients. Serve over fresh salad greens.

Orange-Ginger Vinaigrette

⅔ cup fresh orange juice
2   tablespoons olive oil
2   tablespoons brown rice vinegar
1   teaspoon prepared yellow mustard
1   tablespoon grated fresh ginger root
¼ teaspoon sea salt, or to taste

Combine all ingredients in jar with tight-fitting lid; shake vigorously.

Sesame Salt

1½ cups sesame seeds (21 tablespoons)
1   tablespoon sea salt

Rinse sesame seeds in cool water; drain with fine mesh sieve. Toast salt in dry skillet over medium-high 1 minute; grind to a fine powder in a surbachi or mortar and pestle.

Toast sesame seeds in dry skillet over medium heat 1 to 2 minutes or until seeds begin to pop. Reduce heat to low; toast until golden, stirring to prevent burning. Grind with sea salt using a surbachi or mortar and pestle; pulverize until grainy. *Do not overgrind or it will become a paste.* Store in an air-tight container.

Wakame-Sesame Seasoning

1   6-8" strip dried wakame
¼   cup toasted sesame seeds

Dry roast wakame on ungreased cookie sheet in 400°F oven 5 minutes or until dark and crisp. Grind into a fine powder in food processor or blender. Add sesame seeds; grind into powder *(do not overgrind)*. Store in air-tight container.

Horseradish Sauce

8   ounces silken tofu, drained
2   tablespoons fresh lemon juice
1½-2 tablespoons prepared white horseradish
1   tablespoon olive oil (optional)
1   clove garlic, minced (optional)
1   tablespoon minced or grated onion
½   teaspoon sea salt

Purée all ingredients in blender or food processor until smooth. Warm in small saucepan over low heat or chill. Serve with poached fish.

Variation: For Horseradish-Dill Sauce, prepare recipe as above. Stir in 2 tablespoons chopped fresh dill weed while warming in saucepan.

Miso-Almond Butter Sauce

1   tablespoon brown rice miso
1   tablespoon almond butter
1   cup warm water

In medium saucepan, blend miso and almond butter with fork. Slowly whisk in water until smooth. Place over low heat, stirring constantly, until warm (do not boil). Serve over steamed vegetables.

Tahini Dressing

¾ cup water
¼ cup tahini
2 tablespoons brown rice vinegar
1 - 2 tablespoons umeboshi paste
¼ teaspoon shoyu

Whisk together or purée all ingredients until smooth. Pour over peeled and seeded chopped cucumbers and tomatoes for a Jerusalem Salad.

Peanut Miso Sauce

4 tablespoons miso
4 tablespoons water
3 tablespoons rice syrup
2 tablespoons natural peanut butter
1 clove garlic, crushed
1 teaspoon grated fresh ginger root

Purée all ingredients in blender or food processor until smooth. Serve over sautéed tofu slices or steamed vegetables.

Mushroom-Kuzu Sauce

   Canola or olive oil (optional)
½ pound mushrooms, sliced
1 pinch sea salt
1 tablespoon kuzu
1 cup cold Basic Vegetable Stock (recipe page 60) OR water
1 tablespoon shoyu
¼ teaspoon dried thyme OR ¼ teaspoon garlic power

Lightly coat the bottom of skillet with oil; place over high heat. Sauté mushrooms 3 minutes; sprinkle with salt. Cover; reduce heat to low and cook 2 minutes. Remove from heat; set aside.

Recipe continued following page

In medium saucepan, dissolve kuzu in cool vegetable stock; add shoyu. Simmer over low heat 5 minutes, stirring constantly to prevent lumps from forming. Stir in mushrooms; simmer 1 minute. Serve hot over cooked grains or pasta.

Basic Brown Sauce

4   tablespoons unbleached flour
2   cups water, divided
1 - 2 tablespoons canola or olive oil
4   green onions, chopped
¼   teaspoon sea salt (optional)
1-2 tablespoons shoyu
¼   teaspoon garlic powder OR any desired seasonings or herbs

Toast flour in dry skillet until golden and gives off a nutty aroma. Remove from heat. Whisk flour together with 1 cup water in small bowl; set aside. Coat heated bottom of large skillet with oil; place over high heat. Sauté green onions 2 minutes; add 1 cup water and salt. Simmer over low heat; whisk in flour-water mixture. Simmer 3 minutes or until sauce starts to thicken. Stir in shoyu and garlic; simmer 3 minutes. Serve over sautéed tempeh slices, if desired.

Cranberry Sauce

1   bar agar
    Cool water
3   tablespoons arrowroot
3   cups apple juice, divided
1   pound fresh cranberries
2   oranges, peeled, sectioned, and sliced into thirds
1   tablespoon orange zest (outermost part of peel)
2   tablespoons brown rice syrup

Soak agar bar in water according to package directions. Squeeze our water; break bar into small pieces. Dissolve arrowroot in 1 cup apple juice; place in large saucepan with cranberries and remaining 2 cups juice. Simmer 20 minutes over low heat or until mixture is clear and thickened, stirring frequently to prevent any lumps from forming. Stir in agar pieces; simmer agar until dissolved. Stir in orange pieces, orange zest, and rice syrup; simmer 3 minutes or until heated through. Serve over pancakes or brown rice pudding.

SEA VEGETABLES

Arame and Cabbage Sauté

1   large onion, cut in half and sliced into half-moons
     Olive oil
1   cup dried arame, rinsed, soaked according to package
     directions, and drained
2   cups shredded napa cabbage
     Water
1-2 tablespoons shoyu
1-2 tablespoons mirin
½-1 teaspoon sesame oil
     Toasted sesame seeds OR fresh lemon juice

Lightly coat the bottom of large skillet with oil; place over high heat. Sauté
onion 5 minutes or until golden; reduce heat. Stir in arame; cover and cook
3 minutes. Stir in cabbage; sprinkle with a few drops water. Cover and cook
20 minutes. Stir in shoyu and mirin; cook 1 minute. Just before serving,
sprinkle with sesame seeds or lemon juice.

Arame, Broccoli, and Carrot Salad

¾   cup dried arame, rinsed, soaked according to package
     directions, and drained
     untoasted sesame oil
4   cups broccoli florets
1   cup julienned carrots
4   tablespoons shoyu
4   tablespoons fresh lemon juice
4   tablespoons brown rice vinegar
1   teaspoon mustard powder

Lightly coat the bottom of large skillet with olive oil; place over high heat.
Stir in arame; reduce heat to low. Sauté arame 10 minutes; remove from
skillet to large serving bowl. Recoat skillet with olive oil; sauté broccoli with
carrots 7 minutes or until crisp-tender. Remove from skillet and toss with
arame; let cool until just barely warm.

In a jar with a tight-fitting lid, combine shoyu, lemon juice, vinegar, mustard
powder, and sesame oil; shake vigorously. Pour over vegetable mixture; toss
lightly. Serve warm or chilled.

Arame with Miso-Almond Sauce over Soba

¼ cup miso
1 tablespoon almond butter
   Canola oil
1 onion, halved and sliced into half-moons
1 clove garlic, crushed
1 teaspoon grated fresh ginger root
1 cup dried arame, rinsed, soaked according to package
   directions, and drained
   Water
1 tablespoon toasted sesame seeds
6 ounces firm tofu, drained, crumbled
1 cup pea pods, trimmed and sliced in half on a diagonal
1 tablespoon chopped fresh basil
8 ounces dried soba, cooked and drained

In small saucepan, blend miso with almond butter with fork until smooth. Place over low heat, stirring often. Keep warm.

Lightly coat the bottom of large skillet with oil; place over high heat. Sauté onion 4 minutes or until translucent; stir in garlic, ginger, and arame. Sauté 3 minutes; sprinkle with a few drops of water. Cover and reduce heat to low; cook 15 minutes. Stir in sesame seeds, tofu, pea pods, and basil; cook 3 minutes. Add a few more drops of water, if necessary. Remove from heat.

In large serving bowl, top cooked soba with arame mixture. Spoon miso-almond sauce over vegetables and pasta. Serve immediately.

Arame with Mirin and Lime

1 large onion, sliced into rings
   Olive oil
¾ cup dried arame, rinsed, soaked according to package
   directions, and drained
½ cup fresh corn kernels
   Water
1 tablespoon shoyu
2 tablespoons chopped fresh cilantro
1 tablespoon mirin

Recipe continued following page

1   tablespoon fresh lime juice
1   pinch cayenne pepper

Lightly brush the bottom of large skillet with oil; place over high heat. Sauté onion 4 minutes or until translucent or water "sauté" the onion. Stir in arame and corn. Add enough water to cover; reduce heat to low. Cover and cook 20 minutes.

In small bowl, mix together shoyu, cilantro, mirin, lime juice, and cayenne; pour over arame mixture. Toss gently to coat; remove from heat. Let stand 15 minutes to blend flavors. Reheat over a low flame before serving, if desired.

Kombu Condiment

7   strips kombu
     Water
1/3 cup sake
1   tablespoon brown rice syrup
1/3 cup shoyu

In small bowl, soak kombu in enough water to cover until softened; drain. Cut softened kombu into 1-inch pieces; place in medium saucepan. Add enough water to cover; simmer over low heat 20 minutes. Stir in sake and rice syrup; simmer, uncovered, 15 minutes. Add shoyu in a slow stream, stirring constantly. Simmer over low heat about 1 hour or until all liquid is absorbed. Serve alongside Asian dishes or rice.

Kombu Logs

2   ribbons kombu, softened in water, drained
1   large carrot, cut lengthwise into quarters
1   large burdock root, cut lengthwise into quarters
     Kanpyo strips (dried gourd), softened in water, drained
     Shoyu
1   tablespoon fresh grated ginger root
     Mirin

Spread softened kombu on flat surface. Arrange half of carrot and burdock quarters along the length of 1 kombu ribbon. Roll up tightly, securing ends and center by tying kanpyo strips around. Repeat with remaining kombu ribbons and vegetables, and kanpyo.

Place kombu logs on bottom of large soup pot; add enough water to cover. Simmer over low heat 1 hour or until tender, adding additional water if necessary. Season with shoyu, ginger, and mirin; simmer 7 minutes. Carefully remove kombu logs from pot; slice into ½-inch rounds. Arrange slices cut-sides-up on serving platter; serve warm.

Hiziki Salad

Sesame Dressing (recipe follows on page 164)
½ cup dried hiziki, rinsed, soaked, and drained
Water
1 pinch sea salt
16 ounces firm tofu, drained, crumbled
4 green onions, minced
⅓ cup grated carrot

Prepare Sesame Dressing; set aside.

Chop hiziki into 1-inch pieces; place in medium soup pot. Add enough water to cover; simmerwith salt over low heat 20 minutes. Drain; allow to cool to room temperature.

Meanwhile, parboil the tofu in water in small saucepan 3 minutes. Place tofu in a strainer and with back of a spoon press out any excess water. In large serving bowl, combine tofu with hiziki, green onions, and carrot; toss with dressing. Cover; refrigerate 1 hour to blend flavors. Serve chilled or at room temperature.

SESAME DRESSING

2   tablespoons toasted sesame oil
2   tablespoons shoyu
1   tablespoon fresh lemon juice
1   clove garlic, minced
1   teaspoon prepared yellow mustard

Whisk together all ingredients in small bowl until well blended.

Hiziki-Mushroom Sauté

¾   cup dried hiziki, rinsed, soaked, and drained
    Olive oil or canola oil
4   dried shiitake mushrooms, soaked according to package
    directions and drained, knobby stems removed, caps sliced
    Water
1   tablespoon shoyu
4   ounces firm tofu, drained, cubed (optional)
4   green onions, finely chopped
1   ear sweet corn, kernels removed (optional)
2   teaspoons balsamic vinegar (optional)

Lightly coat the bottom of large skillet with oil; place over high heat. Sauté hiziki and mushrooms 3 minutes; reduce heat to low. Add enough water to cover; cover skillet and cook 45 minutes. Stir in tofu, green onions, and corn; cook 3 minutes. Stir in vinegar if desired; serve immediately.

Hiziki with Onions and Mushrooms

1¼ ounces dried hiziki, rinsed, soaked, and drained
    water
    toasted sesame oil
1   medium onion, chopped
10 mushrooms, sliced
1   pinch sea salt

1   tablespoon sake
1   tablespoon shoyu

Place hiziki in medium saucepan; add enough water to cover. Simmer, covered, over low heat 30 minutes or until tender. Drain.

Meanwhile, lightly coat the bottom of large skillet with olive oil; place over high heat. Sauté onion 4 minutes or until translucent; stir in mushrooms. Reduce heat to low; sprinkle with salt and cover. Sauté 5 minutes or until mushrooms are tender; stir in sake and shoyu. Cook 2 minutes; stir in cooked hiziki and sesame oil. Heat 2 minutes; serve hot.

Savory Hiziki Tart

1   large onion, minced
     Olive oil
2   cloves garlic, crushed
2   cups sliced deribbed kale
¼   cup dried hiziki, rinsed, soaked, and drained
¼   teaspoon EACH: dried basil, cumin, sea salt
1   cup Basic Vegetable Stock (recipe page 60) OR water
3   tablespoons arrowroot
16   ounces firm tofu, drained, crumbled
4   tablespoons almond butter OR toasted tahini
2   tablespoons miso
1   unbaked 9-inch pastry pie crust

Preheat oven to 350°F.

Lightly coat the bottom of large skillet with oil; place over high heat. Sauté onion and garlic 4 minutes or until translucent; reduce heat to low. Stir in kale, hiziki, basil, cumin, and sea salt; cover and steam 8 minutes.

Meanwhile, dissolve arrowroot in cooled vegetable stock. mix with tofu, almond butter, and miso in food processor or blender; blend until smooth.

Spoon hiziki mixture into prepared pie crust; spread evenly. Spread tofu mixture over hiziki mixture; do not blend. Bake 35 to 40 minutes or until golden. Let stand 5 minutes before cutting into slices and serving.

Greens Rolled in Nori

2   bunches watercress, or other leafy green vegetable
    (such as collard or mustard greens)
    Water
1   pinch sea salt
2 - 3 sheets toasted nori

Wash greens thoroughly under cool water. Bring about 3 inches water and salt to a rolling boil in a large soup pot. Blanch greens, 1 bunch at a time, for 2 minutes or until bright green and tender. Drain in colander; rinse with cool water to stop cooking process. Press out any excess water.

Divide greens among nori; roll each sheet into a log. Slice logs into 2- to 3-inch pieces. Serve with Shoyu-Ginger Dipping Sauce (recipe page 150).

FISH*

*Dispensation Food — for those requiring a transition from a meat-based diet or for specific health needs — not necessary for complete nutrition

Grilled Tuna Salad

1   pound fresh tuna, cut into 3 fillets
4   tablespoons sake
4   tablespoons shoyu
1   tablespoon ginger juice
2   teaspoons sesame oil, toasted or light
    Olive oil or canola oil
3   tablespoons brown rice or raspberry vinegar
1   clove garlic, crushed
1   pinch sea salt
    Chopped Romaine lettuce

Place tuna filets in glass baking dish. In small bowl, whisk together sake, shoyu, ginger juice, and sesame oil; pour over tuna. Turn tuna over to coat; marinate no longer than 10 minutes. Remove filets from dish; discard marinade.

Lightly coat heated bottom of large skillet with oil; place over high heat. Sear filets 30 seconds per side for medium-rare. Remove from heat. Slice each filet into thin strips; cool until barely warm.

In small bowl, whisk together 2 tablespoons olive oil, vinegar, garlic, and salt; toss with romaine lettuce in large salad bowl; top with grilled tuna. Serve warm; toss lightly after presenting.

Sweet and Sour Salmon with Peapods

6   cups water
¼   cup shoyu
¼   cup brown rice vinegar
1   large onion, cut in half and sliced into half-rings
2   teaspoons rice syrup
2   cloves garlic, crushed
2   pounds salmon, cut into filets
½   pound fresh peapods, trimmed
1   tablespoon chopped fresh cilantro

In large skillet, combine water, shoyu, vinegar, onion, rice syrup, and garlic. Cover and bring to a boil over high heat. Reduce heat to low and simmer 15 to 20 minutes or until onions are tender. Carefully place salmon filets on top of onions in skillet; cover and steam 4 minutes. Add peapods; steam 2 minutes until crisp-tender. Remove from heat; garnish with cilantro. Serve immediately.

Whole Steamed Fish

2 tablespoons shoyu
1 tablespoon toasted sesame oil
1 clove garlic, crushed
1 tablespoon grated fresh ginger root
¼ teaspoon sea salt
1 whole white-fleshed fish (1½ to 2 pounds), cleaned
3 green onions, finely chopped
¼ cup chopped fresh cilantro (optional)

In small bowl, whisk together shoyu, sesame oil, garlic, ginger, and salt. Brush inside and outside of fish with shoyu mixture. Cut several slits in skin on each side of fish; stuff green onions into slits. Pour any remaining shoyu mixture into slits.

Place fish in basket of steamer over boiling water; steam 10 minutes. Turn off heat and let steam 5 minutes. Garnish with cilantro, if desired.

Oven-Poached Sea Bass or Salmon

1 large onion, chopped
   Olive oil
3 cloves garlic, crushed
1 leek, rinsed thoroughly and chopped
1 stalk celery, chopped
¼ teaspoon sea salt
3 cups Basic Fish Stock (recipe page 77)
2 cups dry white wine
3-4 pounds sea bass (or salmon), cut into filets, reserving the bones
2 tablespoons chopped fresh chives

Recipe continued following page

Preheat oven to 400°F. Lightly coat heated bottom of large skillet with oil; place over high heat. Sauté onion 4 minutes or until translucent; reduce heat to low. Stir in garlic, leek, celery, and salt; sauté 2 minutes. Add fish stock and wine; simmer 15 minutes.

Place filets in 9 x 12-inch glass baking dish; strain stock mixture over filets. Cover with foil; bake 8 minutes or until barely done. Remove from oven; let stand 5 minutes (fish will continue to cook while standing).

Remove filets to individual serving plates; garnish with chives. Serve with Tofu-Dill Sauce (recipe page 175).

Stuffed Rainbow Trout with Tofu Sauce

	Tofu Sauce (recipe follows)
1	large onion, finely chopped
1	tablespoon olive or Canola oil, divided
3	cloves garlic, divided, crushed
1	pound fresh spinach, thoroughly rinsed and drained, trimmed and chopped
¼	teaspoon sea salt, or to taste
12	mushrooms, chopped
1	cup cooked wild rice (optional)
2	ounces sliced almonds
1	whole rainbow trout (about 5 pounds), cleaned and boned

Prepare Tofu Sauce; keep warm. Preheat broiler.

Lightly coat heated bottom of large skillet with ½ tablespoon oil; place over high heat. Sauté onion and 2 cloves garlic 4 minutes or until translucent; reduce heat to low. Stir in spinach and salt; cover and cook 3 minutes. Remove spinach mixture to large bowl; recoat skillet with ½ tablespoon oil. Place over low heat. Sauté mushrooms 5 minutes or until tender. Stir in spinach mixture, rice, and almonds; remove from heat.

Lightly rub inside and outside of trout with remaining 1 clove garlic and salt; stuff with spinach mixture. Carefully skewer fish closed. Broil, about 3 inches from heat, 4 minutes. Carefully turn fish over and broil another 4 minutes. Place stuffed bass on large serving platter; remove skewers. Serve with warm Tofu Sauce.

TOFU SAUCE

6   ounces silken tofu, drained
2   tablespoons olive oil (optional)
1   tablespoon grated fresh onion
1   teaspoon umeboshi paste

Purée ingredients in blender or food processor. Heat in double-boiler until hot.

Sautéed Trout

1   teaspoon dried oregano
½   teaspoon EACH: dried thyme, cumin
¼   teaspoon EACH: sea salt, white pepper
1   pinch cayenne pepper
1½   pounds trout filets
1   tablespoon olive oil
     Lemon slices

In small bowl, combine oregano, thyme, cumin, salt, white pepper, and cayenne. Press spice mixture into both sides of trout filets.

In large, heavy skillet, heat oil over high heat. Sauté filets 1 minute on each side to brown; reduce heat to low. Cover and cook 3 to 4 minutes. Serve with lemon slices.

Orange-Marinated Fish

1   cup orange juice
¼   cup sake
3   tablespoons olive oil (optional)
3   cloves garlic, crushed
¼   cup minced shallots
1   tablespoon grated orange zest (outermost part of peel)
½   teaspoon EACH: dried thyme, rosemary, sea salt
1   pinch pepper
6   whitefish filets

Recipe continued following page

In large non-metallic bowl, combine juice, sake, oil, garlic, shallots, zest, thyme, rosemary, salt, and pepper. Add filets, turning to coat. Cover and marinate 45 minutes. Drain fish; reserve marinade. Simmer reserved marinade in small saucepan over medium heat until reduced by half; keep warm.

Meanwhile, heat broiler or grill. Broil filets 5 minutes or until fish flakes slightly when tested with fork. Spoon orange sauce over filets; serve immediately.

Grilled Striped Bass with Lime-Mustard Marinade

6 striped bass filets
2 medium onions, halved and sliced into half-moons
3 tablespoons fresh lime juice
2 tablespoons olive oil
4 cloves garlic, crushed
2 tablespoons prepared yellow mustard
2 tablespoons EACH: chopped fresh basil, tarragon, and
   parsley OR ¼ teaspoon dried
1 teaspoon grated lime peel
1 teaspoon capers
¾ -1 teaspoon sea salt

Place filets in glass baking dish; arrange onions over fillets. In medium bowl, combine remaining ingredients; pour over fish and onions. Cover and marinate in refrigerator 1½ hours, turning twice.

Drain fish; reserve marinade with onions. Simmer reserved marinade and onions in small saucepan over medium heat until reduced by half and onions are tender; keep warm.

Meanwhile, heat grill or broiler. Grill filets 4 minutes; turn over. Grill 3 minutes or until fish just flakes when tested with fork. Spoon marinade with onions over fish; garnish with lemon wedges, if desired.

Rainbow Trout Dijon

6   rainbow trout filets
    Olive oil
¼   teaspoon sea salt
1   cup coarsely ground almonds
6   green onions, minced
¼   cup dry white wine
2   tablespoons prepared dijon mustard
6   ounces silken tofu, drained
1   teaspoon umeboshi paste

Preheat oven to 350°F. Lightly oil 9 x 12-inch baking dish; set aside.

Brush filets with oil on both sides; sprinkle with salt. Press almonds evenly onto both sides of filets; place in prepared baking dish. Bake 8 to 10 minutes of until fish flakes slightly when tested with fork. Remove to serving platter.

Meanwhile, lightly coat heated bottom of medium saucepan with oil; place over medium heat. Sauté green onions 2 minutes. Stir in wine and mustard; simmer 3 minutes. Blend tofu and umeboshi in small bowl with fork; whisk into saucepan. Simmer 3 minutes; spoon over trout filets. Serve immediately.

Adriatic-Style Red Snapper

2-4 tablespoons olive oil
    Juice of 1 lemon
4   tablespoons chopped fresh basil OR ½ teaspoon dried
2   tablespoons chopped fresh parsley
¼   teaspoon dried thyme
3 - 4 cloves garlic, crushed
    Sea salt
3   pounds red snapper, cut into filets
    Lemon slices

In large glass baking dish, whisk together oil, lemon juice, basil, parsley, thyme, and garlic. Sprinkle both sides of filets with salt; place skin-side-up in marinade. Cover and refrigerate 1 hour.

Recipe continued following page

Heat broiler. Drain snapper filets; discard marinade. Broil filets, skin-side-down, 3 inches from heat source, 5 minutes or until fish flakes slightly when tested with fork. Serve garnished with lemon slices.

Thai-Style White Fish

¼   cup shoyu
    juice from ½ lime
½   cup chopped fresh cilantro
2   tablespoons olive oil
1   tablespoon grated fresh ginger root
2   cloves garlic, crushed
1   pinch black pepper
3   pounds white fish, cut into filets

Preheat broiler or grill.

In large glass bowl, whisk together lime juice, cilantro, ginger, garlic, and pepper. Pour over fish filets in glass baking dish just prior to broiling. Broil filets 8 minutes or until fish flakes slightly when tested with fork, turning after 4 minutes. Serve immediately.

Fish Mousse with Tofu-Dill Sauce

    Tofu-Dill Sauce (recipe follows)
1   tablespoon agar flakes or 1 bar agar
4   cups Basic Vegetable Stock (recipe page 60) OR
    water
8   ounces silken tofu, drained
1   tablespoon fresh lemon juice
1   tablespoon grated fresh onion
1   tablespoon prepared white horseradish
1   teaspoon sea salt
2   cups cubed cooked fish
2   teaspoons umeboshi paste
    Olive oil
    Fresh parsley sprigs

Prepare Tofu-Dill Sauce; refrigerate.

In small saucepan over low heat, simmer agar in vegetable stock until dissolved. Remove from heat; cool to room temperature.

In food processor or blender, combine tofu, lemon juice, onion, horseradish and salt; process until smooth. Add cooled agar mixture, fish, and umeboshi; process until smooth.

Lightly coat 6-cup mold with oil; pour fish mixture into mold. Loosely cover with waxed paper; refrigerate 4 to 6 hours or until set.

To unmold mousse, place mold in warm water halfway up sides for 30 seconds. Invert mousse onto serving platter; remove mold. Garnish with fresh parsley. Serve with Tofu-Dill Sauce.

Tofu-Dill Sauce

```
8   ounces silken tofu, drained
3   tablespoons fresh lemon juice
3   tablespoons fresh dill weed
1   green onion, minced
1   pinch sea salt
1   pinch white pepper
1   tablespoon grated onion
1   clove garlic, crushed
```

In blender or food processor; purée all ingredients until smooth.

SWEETS

Dried Fruit Compote

1   cup water
1   cup apple juice
1   cup sliced dried pitted apricots
1   cup sliced dried apples
½   cup raisins
1   pinch sea salt
2   cinnamon sticks OR ½ teaspoon ground cinnamon
    Granola (recipe follows) OR prepared fat-free granola

Simmer all ingredients except granola in large covered soup pot over low heat until fruit is soft, about 20 minutes. Sprinkle with granola; serve warm or chilled.

Granola

2   cups old-fashioned rolled oats (not instant)
1   cup toasted whole-wheat pastry crumbs
½   cup slivered almonds OR toasted sunflower meats
2   teaspoons ground cinnamon
½   teaspoon sea salt
½   cup brown rice syrup OR brown rice syrup powder
¼   cup canola oil
1   tablespoon maple syrup
1   teaspoon vanilla
⅓   cup raisins (optional)

Preheat oven to 325°F. Lightly oil a large cookie sheet.

In large bowl, combine oats, toasted pastry crumbs, almonds, cinnamon, and salt. In small bowl, combine rice syrup, oil, maple syrup, and vanilla; pour over oat mixture. Toss lightly to coat. Spread mixture evenly onto prepared cookie sheet; bake approximately 20 minutes. Stir in raisins with metal spatula, if desired; bake 10 minutes. Remove to wire rack; lightly separate with a fork (granola will become crispy as it cools).

Bulgur Muffins

¼ cup boiling water
4   tablespoons bulgur
1   cup whole wheat pastry flour
1   teaspoon baking powder
¼ teaspoon cinnamon
1   pinch sea salt
6   tablespoons brown rice syrup
4   tablespoons maple syrup
1   egg, lightly beaten, OR egg substitute
⅓ cup vanilla-flavored soy milk
2   tablespoons canola oil
1   teaspoon orange zest (outermost part of peel)

Preheat oven to 400°F. Lightly oil 12 small muffin cups.

Pour boiling water over bulgur in small bowl; cover and let stand 5 minutes. Drain off any excess water.

In large bowl, combine flour, baking powder, cinnamon, salt, and bulgur. In small bowl, combine rice syrup, maple syrup, egg, soy milk, oil, and orange zest; pour into flour mixture. Mix only until just combined; spoon into prepared muffin cups ½ full. Bake 20 minutes or until toothpick inserted near centers comes out clean.

Fruit Kanten (Fruit Gel)

1   bar agar OR 3½ tablespoons agar flakes
3 ½ cups fruit juice (any flavor)
1   pinch sea salt
½-¾ cup fresh fruit slices

Soak agar bar under cool water. Squeeze out excess water and shred over fruit juice. Add salt. Simmer mixture in medium saucepan over low heat 3 to 5 minutes or until agar is completely dissolved. Stir in fruit slices; pour into a gel mold or container. Refrigerate 3 hours or until set; unmold. Garnish as desired.

Profiteroles

Vanilla Malted Cream, Amasake Cream, OR Almond
Cream (recipes follow)
Berry Sauce (recipe follows)
½   cup unbleached pastry flour
½   cup whole wheat pastry flour
¼   teaspoon sea salt
1   cup water
7   tablespoons Canola oil
4   eggs (from free-range hens), at room temperature

Prepare desired filling and Berry Sauce. Preheat oven to 400°F.

Sift the flour and sea salt together. Bring water and oil to a boil and remove immediately from heat. Add flour mixture all at once; beat vigorously until dough leaves sides of pan and forms a smooth ball. Remove from heat; let stand 2 minutes. Return to the stove for another minute. Beat in eggs, one at a time. Drop heaping tablespoon of dough, 2 inches apart, onto lightly oiled cookie sheets. Bake 10 minutes. *Reduce oven temperature to 325°F.* Continue baking 25 minutes or until golden brown. *(Do not open oven door during baking.)* The puffs should have a hollow sound when tapped lightly. Cool completely on wire racks. Cut profiteroles in half horizontally with serrated knife. Remove soft dough from center of puffs; discard. Fill puffs with desired filling; replace tops. Spoon Berry Sauce over tops.

VANILLA MALTED CREAM

4 ½ tablespoons agar flakes
2   cups malted vanilla-flavored soy milk
1   tablespoon almond butter
1   tablespoon maple syrup
1   tablespoon vanilla

Simmer agar in soy milk in medium saucepan over low heat until agar is completely dissolved, about 5 minutes. Remove from heat; let cool to room temperature. Refrigerate 1 hour or until set. Blend in almond butter, maple syrup, and vanilla until creamy. Refrigerate until ready to use.

Amasake Cream

8   ounces almond-flavored amasake
½   bar agar, rinsed, squeezed dry, and shredded
1   pinch sea salt
1   teaspoon vanilla

Bring amasake and shredded agar just to a boil over high heat in medium saucepan. Reduce heat to low; add salt and simmer 5 minutes or until agar is completely dissolved. Remove from heat; let cool to room temperature. Refrigerate 1 hour or until set. Blend in vanilla until creamy. Refrigerate until ready to use.

Almond Cream

2   cups blanched almonds
2   cups water
²/₃ cup brown rice syrup
1-2 tablespoons maple syrup
1   pinch sea salt
1½ bars agar, rinsed, squeezed dry, and shredded OR 4
     tablespoons agar flakes
2   teaspoons vanilla

Blend almonds and water in blender or food processor until smooth. Strain almond purée to remove any solids; discard solids. In medium saucepan, combine almond liquid, rice syrup, maple syrup, salt, and shredded agar. Bring to just to a boil over high heat; reduce heat to low and simmer 5 minutes or until agar is completely dissolved. Remove from heat; let cool to room temperature. Refrigerate 1 hour or until set. Blend in vanilla until creamy. Refrigerate until ready to use.

BERRY SAUCE

¾   cup berry juice (any flavor)
1   tablespoon kuzu, dissolved in 2 tablespoons water
1   pinch sea salt
1   pint blueberries*, rinsed and drained
3   tablespoons blueberry syrup or brown rice syrup

In medium saucepan, simmer berry juice, kuzu mixture, and salt 3 minutes, stirring often to prevent lumps from forming. Stir in blueberries and syrup; simmer 3 minutes or until slightly thickened.

*Strawberries or another berry may be substituted for blueberries.

Rice Pudding

2   cups short grain brown rice, rinsed and drained
2   cups apple juice
1   cup water
1   pinch sea salt
¼   cup raisins or currants
¼   cup malted vanilla-flaovred soy milk
2   teaspoons vanilla
2   tablespoons almond butter
2   tablespoons rice syrup or maple syrup
½   teaspoon ground cinnamon

Bring rice, juice, water, and salt to a boil in large saucepan over high heat; cover and reduce heat to low. Cook 45 minutes or until all liquid is absorbed. Stir in raisins, soy milk, and vanilla. Simmer over medium heat 15 minutes or until liquid is absorbed. Stir in almond butter, rice syrup, and cinnamon. Simmer 2 to 3 minutes. Serve hot or chilled.

Strawberry Pudding

1   tablespoon kuzu
2   cups almond-flavored amasake
½   bar agar, rinsed, squeezed dry, shredded
1   quart strawberries, hulled and sliced, 4 whole berries
    reserved
2   tablespoons almond butter
1   teaspoon vanilla
1   pinch sea salt
2   tablespoons strawberry syrup or preserves

Dissolve kuzu in amasake in large saucepan. Stir in agar; simmer over low heat until agar is completely dissolved. Cool to room temperature. Purée kuzu mixture with sliced strawberries, almond butter, vanilla, and salt in blender or food processor until smooth. Spoon into 4 parfait or champagne glasses; refrigerate 2 hours or until set. Garnish with reserved whole strawberries. Serve chilled.

Strawberry Mousse

4   cups strawberry juice
1   tablespoon kuzu
2   bars agar, rinsed, squeezed dry, shredded
1   pinch sea salt
3   tablespoons rice syrup
2   tablespoons unsweetened strawberry preserves
1   tablespoon almond butter
1   teaspoon vanilla

Dissolve kuzu in chilled juice in large saucepan. Stir in agar; bring just to a boil over high heat. Stir in salt; reduce heat to low and simmer until agar is completely dissolved, about 5 minutes, stirring often with whisk to prevent lumps from forming. Cool to room temperature; stir in rice syrup, strawberry preserves, almond butter, and vanilla until smooth. Refrigerate 1 hour or until thoroughly chilled. Whip in a blender or food processor until creamy. Chill in refrigerator; serve in parfait glasses.

Sweet Potato Pudding

4   medium sweet potatoes, cooked and peeled
2   tablespoons brown rice syrup
1 -2 tablespoons almond butter
2   teaspoons vanilla
½   teaspoon cinnamon
1   pinch sea salt

Purée all ingredients in blender or food processor until smooth. Serve warm or chilled.

Note: For a thicker pudding, dissolve 1 tablespoon kuzu in 3 tablespoons apple juice. Simmer with puréed sweet potato mixture in large saucepan over low heat until thickened. Refrigerate.

Sweet Potato Muffins

2   cups whole wheat pastry flour
1   tablespoon baking powder
¼   teaspoon nutmeg
¼   teaspoon sea salt
1   large sweet potato, peeled, cooked, mashed
1   cup vanilla-flavored soy milk
7   tablespoons Canola oil
1   egg, lightly beaten
4   tablespoons maple syrup

Preheat oven to 375ºF. Lightly oil 12 small muffin cups. In large bowl, combine flour, baking powder, nutmeg, and salt. In medium bowl, whisk together sweet potato, soy milk, oil, syrup, and egg until smooth; pour into dry ingredients. Mix only until just combined. Spoon into prepared muffin cups ½ full. Bake 20 minutes or until toothpick inserted near centers comes out clean.

Sweet Couscous Tart with Fruit Filling

½-¾ cup shelled walnuts, pecans, OR almonds (optional)
2   cups fruit juice
1   pinch sea salt
¼   teaspoon ground cinnamon
1   cup dry couscous
    Poached fruit (any variety)

Dry roast walnuts on baking sheet in 400°F oven until golden and fragrant, about 10 minutes, stirring twice. Let cool to room temperature; crush nuts with mortar and pestle or food processor.

Bring juice, salt, and cinnamon (if desired) to a boil in medium saucepan over high heat; stir in couscous. Cover; reduce heat to low and simmer 2 to 3 minutes or until liquid is absorbed. Remove from heat. Let stand covered 10 minutes. Stir in nuts. Spoon into 9-inch pie pan; press firmly into bottom and sides with back of spoon to form crust. Cool; fill with poached fruit.

Poached Apple Slices

3   cups apple juice
½ - 1 teaspoon ground cinnamon
1   pinch sea salt
10 Granny Smith apples, 8 Rome Beauty apples, OR 15
    Pippin apples
    Apple Glaze (recipe follows)

In large saucepan, combine apple juice, cinnamon, and salt. Peel, core, and slice apples; add to juice mixture. Bring to a boil over medium heat; simmer about 10 minutes or until tender. Remove apples with a slotted spoon; cool. Arrange apple slices in a cooked pie crust. Top with a thin layer of Apple Glaze.

Apple Glaze

3   cups apple juice
3   tablespoons kuzu
¼   teaspoon cinnamon
1   pinch sea salt

Dissolve kuzu in cool apple juice in large saucepan; stir in cinnamon and salt. Bring to a boil over medium heat; simmer about 5 minutes until mixture thickens and turns transluscent, stirring often to prevent lumps from forming.

Whole Wheat Pie Crust

2   cups whole wheat pastry flour
¼   teaspoon sea salt
7   tablespoons canola oil
7   tablespoons water

Preheat oven to 350°F. Lightly oil 8-inch pie plate.

Combine flour and salt in large bowl. Cut in oil with a pastry blender or 2 knives until coarse crumbs form. Add water, 1 tablespoon at a time, until dough forms a ball. Divide dough in half; roll each half into a ball.

Roll out 1 dough ball between 2 pieces of waxed paper to about ¼-inch thickness. Carefully remove top sheet of waxed paper; invert pastry into prepared pie plate. Remove second sheet of waxed paper; fill as desired. Roll out second dough ball the same as the first; place over filling. Fold edges under; flute. Cut slits or in top crust or prick with a fork to allow steam to escape. Bake according to pie filling directions. Cover edges with foil, if necessary, to prevent overbrowning.

Notes: Do not overhandle pastry or it will toughen.

For a single pie crust, cut recipe in half and bake in a 350°F oven for 5 minutes.

Pressed Oat Crust

¾ cup old-fashioned rolled oats (not instant)
¾ cup whole wheat pastry flour
¼ cup toasted sesame seeds
⅛ teaspoon salt
1 tablespoon brown rice syrup OR barley malt
¼-½ cup Canola oil

Preheat oven to 350°F. Lightly oil a 9-inch pie plate.

Combine all ingredients in large bowl until crumbly; press evenly into prepared pie plate. Bake for 10 minutes or until golden. Let cool to room temperature before filling.

Fruit Filling with Glaze

½ cup apple or pear juice
1 pinch sea salt
6 medium apples OR pears, peeled, cored, and sliced
1 tablespoon kuzu, dissolved in 2 tablespoons fruit juice
¼ teaspoon cinnamon

Bring juice and salt to a boil in large pot over high heat; add fruit slices. Reduce heat to low; simmer 3 to 4 minutes or until fruit is tender. Remove fruit slices with slotted spoon; arrange in prepared tart shell or pie crust.

Stir kuzu mixture into juice mixture; simmer over low heat, stirring constantly, 3 to 4 minutes or until clear and thickened. Stir in cinnamon. Use as a glaze over fruit slices or refrigerate and use as a syrup.

Strawberry Tart with Kuzu Glaze

1 tablespoon kuzu, dissolved in 2 tablespoons fruit juice
1 cup strawberry-apple juice
1 pinch sea salt

2 tablespoons strawberry preserves
1½ pints strawberries, cleaned, hulled, and sliced
1 prebaked tart crust
½ cup slivered almonds
1 whole strawberry

Bring kuzu mixture, juice, and salt to a boil in medium heavy saucepan over high heat; reduce heat to low. Simmer 3 to 4 minutes or until clear and thickened, whisking constantly to prevent lumps from forming. Remove from heat; set aside.

Arrange strawberry sliced in tart shell spiral-fashion starting from outside rim with points facing out. Spoon hot kuzu glaze over strawberries. Top with almonds; place whole strawberry in center for garnish.

Note: Strawberries and glaze can be spooned over chilled amasake custard or pudding.

Pumpkin Pie

2 cups cooked puréed pumpkin
1½ bars agar, soaked, squeezed dry, and shredded
2 cups malted vanilla-flavored soy milk
½ cup rice syrup
2 teaspoons vanilla
¼ teaspoon cinnamon
1 pinch sea salt
1 prebaked 9-inch pie shell
½ cup pecan halves

Combine pumpkin, agar, and soy milk in large heavy saucepan; bring to a boil over high heat, stirring often. Remove from heat; stir in rice syrup, vanilla, cinnamon, and salt. Let cool to room temperature; refrigerate until set. Purée in food processor or blender; pour into prepared pie shell. Garnish with pecan halves. Serve chilled or at room temperature.

Pumpkin Tart with Glazed Pecans

2   cups cooked puréed pumpkin
1   egg, lightly beaten, OR egg substitute
1   cup vanilla-flavored soy milk
1¼ cup rice syrup, divided
1   teaspoon cinnamon
⅛ teaspoon nutmeg
1   pinch sea salt
1   prebaked 9-inch tart shell
½   cup pecan halves

Preheat oven to 400°F.

In large bowl, whisk together pumpkin, egg, soy milk, 1 cup rice syrup, cinnamon, nutmeg, and salt. Pour into prepared tart shell; bake 15 minutes. *Reduce oven temperature to 375°F.* Bake 45 minutes or until set; let cool to room temperature.

Meanwhile, in small heavy saucepan over medium heat, bring remaining ¼ cup rice syrup to a boil. Remove from heat; stir in pecan halves. Arrange glazed pecans around the edge of pumpkin tart.

Lemon Custard

1   bar agar, soaked, squeezed dry, and shredded OR 4
     tablespoons agar, flaked
3   cups apple juice
1   pinch sea salt
2   tablespoons kuzu, dissolved in 4 tablespoons juice
     Juice of 1 lemon
3-4 tablespoons rice syrup
1   tablespoon maple syrup
1   tablespoon almond butter OR 1 tablespoon toasted
     tahini
1   teaspoon vanilla

Bring agar, apple juice, and salt to a boil in large saucepan over high heat; reduce heat to low. Simmer 3 minutes or until agar is dissolved. Stir in kuzu mixture; simmer, stirring constantly, until mixture is clear and thickened. Remove from heat. Cool to room temperature. In small bowl, whisk together lemon juice, rice syrup, maple syrup, almond butter and vanilla; whisk into kuzu mixture. Pour into gel mold or individual parfait glasses; refrigerate until set.

Squash Pie

1   3-pound buttercup squash, baked, peeled, and seeded
1   egg, lightly beaten, OR egg substitute
½   teaspoon ground cinnamon
¼   teaspoon ground nutmeg
1   pinch sea salt
1   cup chilled almond amasake
3   tablespoons kuzu
1   unbaked prepared 9-inch pie shell

Preheat oven to 350°F. Purée squash, egg, cinnamon, nutmeg, and salt in blender or food processor until smooth.

In small saucepan, stir together amasake and kuzu; place over medium heat. Simmer, stirring constantly, until clear and thickened. Remove from heat; let stand 5 minutes. Stir kuzu mixture into squash mixture; pour into prepared pie shell. Bake 30 minutes or until toothpick inserted near center comes out clean. Serve warm or chilled.

Chestnut Purée

¾   cup dried chestnuts, soaked overnight, drained
1   pinch sea salt
3   tablespoons rice syrup, or to taste
1   teaspoon vanilla

In pressure cooker, place chestnuts and enough water to cover. Add salt; cover and bring to pressure over high heat. Reduce heat to low; cook 45 minutes. Drain chestnuts. Purée chestnuts with rice syrup and vanilla in blender or food processor. Use as a pie filling, cream puff, or cake topping.

Chestnut Cream Pie

1½   cups dried chestnuts OR 1¾ cups fresh chestnuts
3   cups water, divided
1   pinch sea salt
½   cup old-fashioned rolled oats (not instant)
2   bars agar, soaked, squeezed dry, and shredded
4   cups apple juice
¼   cup rice syrup
2   tablespoons maple syrup OR ¼ cup barley malt
1   tablespoon vanilla
½   teaspoon fresh lemon juice
1   prebaked 9-inch pie shell
¼   cup slivered toasted almonds

In pressure cooker, place chestnuts in water to cover. Add salt; cover and bring to pressure over high heat. Reduce heat to low; cook 45 minutes. Drain. Meanwhile, bring oats and 1 cup water to a boil in medium saucepan. Cover and simmer for 10 minutes.

In medium saucepan, combine agar and apple juice. Bring to a boil over high heat, stirring often. Reduce heat to low; simmer for 3 to 4 minutes until agar is completely dissolved. Remove from heat; refrigerate until set.

In food blender or processor, blend chestnuts, and oats until smooth. Blend in rice syrup, maple syrup, vanilla, and lemon juice. Pour into prepared pie shell; top with almonds. Refrigerate until ready to serve.

Apple Tart

1   prepared Pressed Oat Crust (recipe page 186)
6   large Golden Delicious apples
     fresh lemon juice
1   tablespoon kuzu, dissolved in 3 tablespoons apple
     juice
½   cup apple juice
½   teaspoon cinnamon
1   pinch sea salt
     Cinnamon Apple Glaze (recipe follows)

Prepare Pressed Oat Crust; set aside.

Peel, core, and slice apples; rub each cut side with lemon juice to prevent browning.

In large saucepan, bring kuzu mixture, apple juice, cinnamon, and salt to a boil over high heat, stirring constantly. Reduce heat to low; simmer until clear and thickened. Remove from heat; stir in apple slices. Let cool to room temperature.

With slotted spoon, arrange apple slices in Pressed Oat Crust spiral-fashion. Spoon Cinnamon Apple Glaze over.

Note: Pears or peaches may be substituted for apples for a delicious variation.

CINNAMON APPLE GLAZE

1	tablespoon kuzu
1	cup cool apple juice
½	teaspoon cinnamon

In small saucepan, dissolve kuzu in juice; stir in cinnamon. Bring to a boil over high heat, stirring constantly; reduce heat to low. Simmer until clear and thickened. Let cool to room temperature.

Oatmeal-Sesame-Raisin Cookies

3	cups old-fashioned rolled oats (not instant)
¾	cup whole wheat pastry flour
½	cup toasted sesame seeds
1	teaspoon baking soda
¾	teaspoon cinnamon
¼	teaspoon sea salt
2/3	cup brown rice syrup
½	cup Canola oil
1	teaspoon vanilla
1/3	cup raisins

Recipe continued following page

Preheat oven to 375°F. Lightly oil 2 cookie sheets.

In large bowl, combine oats, flour, sesame seeds, baking powder, cinnamon, and salt. In medium bowl, combine rice syrup, oil, and vanilla; stir into oat mixture. Stir in raisins.

Drop dough by tablespoonfuls onto prepared cookie sheets. Press flat with moistened tines of fork. Bake 10 minutes or until lightly browned around edges; remove to wire racks. Repeat with remaining dough.

Carob Chip Cookies

1½ cups whole wheat pastry flour
½   cup old-fashioned rolled oats (not instant)
½   teaspoon baking powder
½   teaspoon baking soda
¼   teaspoon sea salt
1   egg, from free-range hen, lightly beaten
½   cup rice syrup
⅓   cup Canola oil
2   tablespoons maple syrup
1   tablespoon vanilla
½   cup carob chips (non-dairy, malt-sweetened)
½   cup chopped pecans OR walnuts (optional)

Preheat oven 375°F. Lightly oil 2 cookie sheets.

In large bowl, combine flour, oats, baking powder, baking soda, and salt. Set aside.

In small bowl, combine egg, rice syrup, oil, maple syrup, and vanilla; stir into flour mixture. Stir in carob chips and pecans until combined.

Drop by tablespoonfuls onto prepared cookie sheets about 1½ inches apart. Bake 10 to 12 minutes or until golden brown. Remove to wire racks; repeat with remaining dough.

Peanut Butter Cookies

1   cup peanut butter
2   tablespoons canola oil
1   cup rice syrup
2   tablespoons maple syrup
1   egg , OR egg substitute
1   teaspoon vanilla
2   cups whole wheat pastry flour
1   teaspoon baking soda
¼   teaspoon sea salt

Preheat oven 350°F. Lightly oil 2 cookie sheets.

Blend peanut butter and oil together in large bowl until creamy. Beat in rice syrup, maple syrup, egg white, and vanilla. Sift together flour, soda, and salt; blend into peanut butter mixture.

Drop dough by tablespoonfuls onto prepared cookie sheets. Press flat with moistened tines of a fork. Bake 10 minutes or until lightly browned around edges; remove to wire racks. Repeat with remaining dough.

Almond-Oat Crisps

2 ½ cups old-fashioned rolled oats (not instant)
½   whole wheat pastry flour
⅓   cup ground almonds
1   teaspoon baking soda
¼   teaspoon sea salt
¾   cup rice syrup
⅓   cup almond butter
1   tablespoon canola oil
½   teaspoon vanilla

Preheat oven 350°F. Lightly oil 2 cookie sheets.

In large bowl, combine oats, flour, ground almonds, baking soda, and salt. Set aside.

Recipe continued following page

In medium bowl, blend together rice syrup, almond butter, oil, and vanilla until creamy; blend into oat mixture. Drop dough by tablespoonfuls onto prepared cookie sheets. Bake 8 to 10 minutes or until golden; remove to wire racks. Repeat with remaining dough.

Carob-Frosted Brownies

1   cup whole wheat pastry flour
½   cup carob powder
1   teaspoon baking powder
¼   teaspoon sea salt
1   egg, from free-range hen, OR egg substitute, lightly beaten
¾   cup rice syrup
½   cup canola oil
2   teaspoons vanilla
    Carob Frosting (recipe follows)

Preheat oven 350°F. Lightly oil 8 x 8-inch baking pan.

In large bowl, combine flour, carob powder, baking powder, and salt. Set aside.

In medium bowl, whisk together egg, rice syrup, oil, and vanilla; beat into carob mixture until smooth. Pour into prepared pan. Bake 40 minutes or until toothpick inserted near center comes out clean. Let cool to room temperature before frosting and cutting into bars.

CAROB FROSTING

½   cup carob chips
1   cup brown rice syrup
¼   cup vanilla-flavored soy milk
2   teaspoons vanilla
1   cup carob powder

Melt carob chips in top of a double boiler over simmering water; whisk until smooth. Whisk in rice syrup, soy milk, egg white, and carob powder until creamy and of spreading consistency.

Popcorn & Peanut Crunch

1   cup brown rice syrup
3   tablespoons canola oil
1   tablespoon almond butter
1   teaspoon vanilla
1   pinch sea salt
10 cups popped popcorn
1-2 cups dry-roasted peanuts

Preheat oven to 300°F. Lightly oil 2 baking sheets.

Combine rice syrup and canola oil in medium heavy saucepan. Bring to soft-ball stage (240°F) over low heat; stir in almond butter, vanilla, and salt.

Meanwhile, combine popcorn and peanuts in large bowl. Carefully pour syrup mixture over, stirring to coat. Spread mixture evenly on prepared baking sheets. Bake 8 to 10 minutes; carefully spread popcorn mixture onto waxed paper. When cool enough to handle, form into balls with lightly oiled hands.

Cornmeal Pudding

8   cups apple juice
2   cups toasted cornmeal
    Zest from 1 lemon (outermost part of peel)
½   cup currants
¼   cup sunflower seeds
¼   cup tahini
½   teaspoon cinnamon
⅛   teaspoon sea salt

Bring apple juice to a boil over high heat in large soup pot. Whisk in cornmeal; reduce heat to low. Stir in remaining ingredients. Simmer, covered, 15 to 20 minutes or until all liquid is absorbed. Stir to prevent any lumps from forming. Cool before serving.

Baked Apples with Filling

4 - 6 tart, firm apples
1   pinch sea salt
2   tablespoons rice syrup
1 - 2 tablespoons currants, or raisins
1 - 2 teaspoons almond butter
¼   teaspoon cinnamon
½   cup water

Preheat oven to 350ºF.

Core apples ¾ down to base to form shell. Place apples in glass baking dish; sprinkle centers with salt.

In a small bowl, combine rice syrup, currants, almond butter, and cinnamon. Evenly fill apple centers with currant mixture; fill baking dish with water. Bake filled apples 25 to 30 minutes or until apples are tender. Remove from baking dish; serve hot.

Apple Crêpes with Caramel Sauce

Crêpes
1   cup whole wheat pastry flour
1½ cups soy milk
1   egg, OR egg substitute, lightly beaten
½   teaspoon vanilla
     Canola oil
Filling
     Poached Apple Slices (recipe page 184)
Caramel Sauce
½   cup rice syrup
¼   cup silken tofu, drained
3   tablespoons maple syrup
1   teaspoon almond butter
1   teaspoon vanilla
1   pinch sea salt

For Crêpes: Sift flour into a large bowl and form a well in center. Add soy milk, egg, and vanilla into well; whisk to form a smooth batter. Allow batter to rest 1 hour. Meanwhile, prepare Poached Apple Slices; set aside.

Brush the bottom of a large skillet or crêpe pan with oil; place over medium heat. Pour ¼ cup batter into skillet, tilting to form an even circle. Cook until golden, about 3 to 4 minutes. Gently lift edge of crêpe with a kinife to check for doneness. With a metal spatula, carefully flip crêpe and cook second side until golden. Remove to wax paper-lined platter. Repeat with remaining batter; separate crepes with wax paper. (Crêpes can be prepared a day or two ahead of time, wrapped in foil, and refrigerated. Reheat wrapped in foil in 350°F oven for 10 minutes.)

For Caramel Sauce: Heat rice syrup in large sauce pan over medium heat just until boiling. Whisk in tofu, maple syrup, almond butter, vanilla, and salt. Simmer 1 minute; remove from heat.

For Assembly: Preheat oven to 350°F. Spoon about ½ cup Poached Apple Slices along center of 1 crêpe. Roll up and place seam-side-down on a lightly oiled baking sheet. Repeat with remaining crêpes and Poached Apple Slices. Cook filled crêpes 15 minutes; remove from oven. Place 2 apple crêpes on individual desert plates; spoon warm Caramel Sauce over. Refrigerate leftovers.

Apple Crisp

Filling
5 - 6 tart, firm apples, peeled, cored, and sliced
2   tablespoons rice syrup powder
1   teaspoon cinnamon
     Canola oil
Topping
2   cups old-fashioned rolled oats (not instant)
½   cup whole wheat pastry flour
²/₃ cup chopped pecans or almonds
8   tablespoons rice syrup powder
1   teaspoon cinnamon
⅛   teaspoon sea salt
¼   cup Canola oil
⅓   cup brown rice syrup

Recipe continued following page

For Filling: Preheat oven to 350°F; lightly oil a glass baking dish. Toss apple slices with brown rice syrup powder and cinnamon; place in prepared baking dish.

For Topping: In large mixing bowl, combine oats, flour, pecans, brown rice syrup powder, cinnamon, and salt. In small bowl combine oil and rice syrup; pour over dry ingredients. Mix until crumbly; sprinkle evenly over apple slices. Bake 35 minutes or until apples are tender and topping is golden.

Apple-Corn Slices

    2   cups cornmeal
    1½   cups cooked couscous
    5 - 6 apples, cored, peeled, and chopped
    ½   teaspoon sea salt
    1   teaspoon cinnamon
    3   cups apple juice
    ¼   cup canola oil
    2   cups boiling water

Preheat oven to 350°F. Lightly oil a glass baking dish.

In large bowl, combine all ingredients except boiling water. Pour boiling water over; mix well. Pour batter into prepared baking dish; bake 20 minutes or until golden. Cool to room temperature and slice into squares.

Carrot Cake

    1½   cups whole wheat pastry flour
    1½   cups unbleached white flour
    2   teaspoons baking powder
    1½   teaspoons cinnamon
    ½   teaspoon baking soda
    ¼   teaspoon mace
    ¼   teaspoon allspice
    1   cup vanilla-flavored soy milk
    ¾   cup canola oil

¾   cup egg substitute OR 1 egg white combined with 2¼
    teaspoons soy milk, and 2 teaspoons canola oil
½   cup rice syrup
¼   cup maple syrup
1   teaspoon vanilla
1   teaspoon rice vinegar
2   cups shredded carrots
¾   cup raisins

Preheat oven to 350°F. Lighlty oil 9 x 13-inch baking dish; set aside.

Into a large bowl, sift together flours, baking powder, cinnamon, baking soda, mace, and allspice. In medium bowl, combine soy milk, oil, egg substitute, rice syrup, maple syrup, vanilla, and vinegar; stir into dry ingredients. Stir in carrots and raisins; mix well.

Pour batter into prepared baking dish; bake 45 to 50 minutes or until a tooth-pick inserted near center comes out clean. Remove to wire rack; cool to room temperature. Garnish with orange kuzu glaze, if desired.

Basic White Cake

2¼ cups unbleached white flour
1   tablespoon baking powder
½   teaspooon baking soda
¼   teaspoon sea salt
1¼ cups soy milk
½   cup rice syrup
1/3 cup PLUS 2 tablespoons canola oil
1/3 cup maple syrup
1   egg, lightly beaten
1   tablespoon vanilla
1   teaspoon rice vinegar
    Desired filling, such as Almond Cream, Amasake
    Custard, or pureed strawberries (see recipes this
    chapter), optional
    Desired topping, such as Strawberry or Blueberry
    Kuzu Glaze or Carob Frosting (see recipes this
    chapter), optional

Recipe continued following page

Preheat oven to 350°F. Lightly oil and flour 2 round cake pans; set aside.

Into large bowl, sift together flour, baking powder, baking soda, and salt. In medium bowl, combine soy milk, rice syrup, oil, maple syrup, egg, vanilla, and vinegar; pour into dry ingredients. Whisk until batter is smooth without any lumps. Pour batter evenly into prepared cake pans; bake 30 to 40 minutes or until tootpick inserted near center comes out clean. Remove to wire racks; let cool to room temperature. Fill and top as desired.

Carob Cake

1½ cups whole wheat pastry flour
1   cup unbleached white flour
½   cup carob powder
¼   cup rice powder
1   tablespoon baking powder
1   teaspoon baking soda
1/8 teaspoon sea salt
1   cup soy milk
½   cup rice syrup
1/3 cup PLUS 2 tablespoons canola oil
1/3 cup maple syrup
1   egg, lightly beaten, OR 1½ teaspoons egg replacer
     mixed with 2 tablespoons water
1   tablespoon vanilla
1   teaspoon rice vinegar
     Desired filling, such as Amasake Cream or Almond
     Cream (see recipes this chapter)
     Desired topping, such as Strawberry Glaze (see recipe
     this chapter)

Preheat oven to 350°F. Lightly oil and flour 2 round cake pans; set aside.

Into a large bowl, sift together flours, carob powder, brown rice powder, baking powder, baking soda, and salt. In medium bowl, combine soy milk, brown rice syrup, oil, maple syrup, egg, vanilla, and brown rice vinegar; pour over dry ingredients. Whisk until batter is smooth without any lumps. Pour batter evenly into prepared cake pans; bake 30 to 40 minutes or until tootpick inserted near center comes out clean. Remove to wire racks; let cool to room temperature. Fill and top as desired.

SEASONAL MENU SUGGESTIONS

Fall Menu Plan

	MONDAY	TUESDAY	WEDNESDAY	THURSDAY	FRIDAY	SATURDAY	SUNDAY
SOUP	Squash Potage	Lentil	Curried Creamy Broccoli	Aduki Bean	Wild Rice Mushroom	Vegetable w/Wakame Strips	Chickpea
GRAIN	Millet/Chickpea Patties in Brown Sauce	Saffron Quinoa	Rice-Stuffed Squash	Polenta w/Mushrooms	(see soup) [Sourdough Bread]	(see protein)	Buckwheat Tabouli
CON-CENTRATED PROTEIN	(see grain)	(see soup)	Braised Tempeh/w mustard Sauce	(see soup)	Talapia Adriatic Style	Tofu Fettucini	(see soup)
VEGETABLES	Veggies a la Greque	Grilled Skewered Veggies	(see protein) Steamed Greens with Ponzu	(see sea veggies)	Composed Salad	Watercress Napa Pinwheels in Lemony Sauce	Spaghetti Squash w/ Sesame
SEA VEGETABLES	(see veggies)	Hiziki with Onions [Nori Strips]		Arame w/Cabbage Saute	(see veggies)	(see soup)	(see veggies)
SWEETS	Apple Crisp	Fruit Compote	Couscous w/Poached Pear Slices	Rice Pudding	Baked Apples	Sweet Potato Muffins	Pumpkin Pie

Winter Menu Plan

	MONDAY	TUESDAY	WEDNESDAY	THURSDAY	FRIDAY	SATURDAY	SUNDAY
SOUP	Bonita Flake	Chickpea Potage	French Onion w/Herbed Croutons	Aduki Bean	Hot and Sour	Yellow Split Pea	Mushroom Barley
GRAIN	Buckwheat Pilaf	Warm Rice with Capers	Millet with Veggies	Soba Rolled in Nori	Saffron Rice (Bread)	Brown Rice with Kuzu	(see soup)
CON-CENTRATED PROTEIN	Lentil Pâté	(see soup)	Black Beans with Hiziki	(see soup)	Stuffed Trout	(see soup)	Seitan-Vegetable Medley
VEGETABLES	Boiled Salad with Wakame	Baked Greens	Squash Slices	Cauliflower Sauté	(see protein)	Savory Onion Tart w/ Steamed Greens	(see protein)
SEA VEGETABLES	(see veggies)	Arame with Mushrooms	(see protein)	(see grain)	(Nori Strips)	(Dulse Sprinkles)	Arame with Onion & Lime
SWEETS	Dried Fruit Compote	Apple Sauce	Amasake Custard	Rice Pudding	Pear-Caramel Tart	Baked Apples	Oatmeal Cookies

Spring Menu Plan

	MONDAY	TUESDAY	WEDNESDAY	THURSDAY	FRIDAY	SATURDAY	SUNDAY
SOUP	Millet-Ginger Parsley	Split Pea w/Croutons	Leek	Minestrone w/Elbows	Creamy Curried Broccoli	Kombu-Bonita Flake w/Snow Peas	Chickpea
GRAIN	Sourdough Bread	Gingered Pasta Salad	Wheat Berries and Barley	Rice Patties	Rice Timbales	(see protein)	Saffron Rice
CONCENTRATED PROTEIN	Lentils Rolled in Cabbage	(see soup)	Tofu-Yong with Kuzu Sauce	(see soup)	Struiped Bass w/Lime Mustard	Quinoa w/Seitan	(see soup)
VEGETABLES	Pressed Cukes	Squash Purée	Grilled Veggies	Steamed Greens w/Vinaigrette	Cauliflower Sauté	Pressed Salad	Steamed Squash Slices
SEA VEGETABLES	Arame with Carrots	(kombu in soup)	Wakame w/Miso	(Dulse Sprinkle)	Carrot-Daikon Salad	Hiziki with Mushrooms	Hiziki Tart
SWEETS	Strawberry Whip	Oat-Almond Cookies	Fruit Crisp	Cranberry-Apple Kanten	Profiteroles	Poached Pears w/Granola	Fruit Couscous Tart

Summer Menu Plan

	MONDAY	TUESDAY	WEDNESDAY	THURSDAY	FRIDAY	SATURDAY	SUNDAY
SOUP	Chilled Carrot Bisque w/Dill	French Onion w/Croutons	Minestrone w/White Beans	Yellow Pea Potage	Chilled Cucumber	Corn Chowder	Split Pea w/Croutons
GRAIN	Basmati with Pumpkin Seeds	Warm Rice with Capers	Pasta with Broccoli & Sun-Dried Tomatoes	Buckwheat Salad	Quinoa Salad	Rice w/Kuzu Whole Wheat Buns	Gingered Pasta Salad
CON-CENTRATED PROTEIN	Chickpea Salad	Seitan Kebabs w/Veggies	(see soup)	(see soup)	Grilled Snapper with Lemon & Oregano	Lentil Patties	(see soup)
VEGETABLES	Kale-Stuffed Onions	Sweet Corn & Pressed Salad	Parsnip Purée	Grilled Veggies	Watercress-Shiitake Sauté	Steamed Greens w/Ponzu Salad	Steamed Carrots
SEA VEGETABLES	(Nori Strips)	Arame with Onions	Wakame-Cuke Salad	Hiziki with Mushrooms	Composed Salad w/Miso Dressing	Arame w/Onions	(see grain)
SWEETS	Poached Pears & Lime Crisp	Raspberry Couscous Tart	Peach Kanten	Fresh Melon & Oatmeal Cookies	Layer Cake w/Strawberry Glaze	Lemon Pudding	Fruit Crisp

Appendix

THE BLOCK NUTRITION PROGRAM
ORIGINS AND RATIONALE

The Block Nutrition Protocol, developed in my husband's clinical practice is a significant component of his comprehensive medical program. Initially it grew out of a macrobiotic approach (now modified to meet specific medical and nutritional standards), which in turn is based on traditional eating patterns which sustained human life until the era of the Industrial Revolution. Traditional diets were commonly composed of whole cereal grains, vegetables, legumes, fruits, nuts, seeds, and some animal products although individual ingredients in daily use might vary among cultures, usually the general configuration of meals was similar.

For instance, if you were to sit down to a dinner in China the primary grain might be rice, whereas suppertime in an ancient Incan home quite possibly featured corn or quinoa. Unfortunately, all of this has changed since the Industrial Revolution. Western countries have progressively switched from wholesome fare to a diet high in saturated fat, protein, and processed foods and low in whole grains and fresh vegetables. Epidemiological reports have linked this westernized diet — this relatively recent style of eating — with a host of degenerative and catastrophic diseases.

Historically, macrobiotic-type diets have been followed in the Orient and other rural regions for thousands of years. At the end of the 19th century, a Japanese army physician, Dr. Sagen Ishizuka, began to investigate the relationship of whole, unadulterated foods to the remediation of sickness, laying the foundation for macrobiotic nutrition. In order to find a cure for a disorder, he first sought to find its source within an individual's diet. Ishizuka emphasized improved physical resistance to disease, rather than symptomatic cures.

As a fundamental principle, Dr. Ishizuka proposed that potassium salts and sodium salts are both antagonistic and complementary to each other in their physiological functions, with potassium salts activating oxidation (the union of a substance with oxygen), and sodium salts inhibiting it. He divided foods into two categories depending on the predominant salt, and observed that the health and physiological functioning of his patients was improved if he adjusted the balance of these two salts in their diet. As a consequence of this and other insights, Dr. Ishizuka theorized that the blood of someone eating grains and vegetables, with their naturally high potassium component, would oxidize well and improve physiological functioning. On the other hand, a diet rich in animal foods (meat, poultry, eggs, dairy products), found to be high in sodium salts, would impair physiological functioning. Through dietary manipulation, Ishizuka sought to correct patients' sodium-potassium imbalances and thus to help restore or improve their health.

In studying the macrobiotic regimen and evaluating it in his clinical practice, Keith did discover numerous areas of agreement, but he also pinpointed specific areas of disagreement and concern. For instance, while the stated intention of practioners may have been to adjust the diet to meet individual, climatic and varying cultural backgrounds and needs, such intentions have only been sporadically realized. To achieve compliance, a nutritional plan should take into account a complete set of biological and social considerations for genuine adaptation between an individual and his or her cultural, geographic, biologic, and social needs. In addition, due to a lack of scientific standards, the macrobiotic program, promoted by lay literature throughout the United States and western Europe, arouses nutritional concerns.

Thus, when Keith designed the Block Nutrition Program, he drew from other nutritional sources and guidelines that are far more complete, nutritionally adequate, and sophisticated than previous macrobiotic formulas. These resources included an extensive review of medical literature, U.S. Department of Agriculture publications, a history and development of dietary exchange lists, nutritional laboratory data, consultations and reviews, evaluations by several dietitians and nutritionists, and the empirical results of more than 15 years of clinical work. Utilizing the information culled from these sources, Dr. Block developed a dietary exchange list—the first semivegetarian one—to assure his patients of optimal nutrition in a program shaped to match their individual needs. In this way, Dr. Block has expanded on a critical principal of Ishizuka—that of helping the body to maintain and restore its internal balance its balance through proper nutrition which is key to good health.

THE PRINCIPAL OF HOMEOSTASIS

Homeostasis, the body's internal balance which is essential to health, is manifested in a number of ways:

Biochemical level: Represented by critical ratios of biochemical elements such as acid/alkaline, sodium/potassium, etc.

Physiological level: Represented by oxygen/carbon dioxide (cardiac and respiratory cycle), intestinal flora and fauna/gastrointestinal functioning, etc.

Nutritional level: For example, positive nitrogen and calcium/phosphorus balance (musculo-skeletal functions).

Geographic-climatic level: Maintaining balance between internal and external environment in terms of body temperature, activity, and ability to respond appropriately to changes in climate.

Conditioning level: A balance between state of health and activity level.

Maintaining homeostasis requires that the body's finite energy stores, represented by adenosine triphosphate (ATP), which is the basic fuel for all cells, be used efficiently to run the various functions that maintain life and health: metabolism, immune responses, respiration, circulation, brain activity, and the like. If the body is subjected to extremes of stress, diet, climate, physical labor, or other activities, a greater proportion of those finite stores, or ATP, must be used to restore homeostasis. While many of these extremes are beyond our control, our diet is one factor that is not. In fact, through proper food choices, preparation, and patterns of eating, we can easily learn not only how to minimize adverse extremes but also how to use them to our benefit.

A diet that places undue stress on the body can have important implications on many levels — particularly for functions, such as the immune system, that require a high level of nutrients and energy to be able to proliferate immune enhancing cells. If an individual's diet consists primarily of foods that are imbalanced and maladaptive in their sodium/potassium, acid/alkaline, or other ratios (too much animal protein, saturated fat, refined sugars), the body must use more of its ATP stores and mineral reserves to metabolize these foods and to restore homeostasis.

On the other hand, a diet as closely balanced as possible — assisting the organism in establishing appropriate nutritional adaptation (environmental homeostasis) — would require far less energy to metabolize and assimilate. As a happy consequence, more energy would be available for other physiological functions, such as the immune system, enabling the body to respond more effectively to internal and external stressors. It is reasonable to assume that such a diet would exert a beneficial effect on an individual's overall health and the maintenance of a strong, resistant state.

With an understanding of homeostasis as a fundamental guide, the Block Nutrition Program has been structured to provide a basically healthy individual with a diet consisting of 50 to 60 percent complex carbohy-drates, a maximum of 25 percent and minimum of 12 percent fat, as needed (primarily from vegetables sources), and the balance of calories coming from protein. The Block Nutrition Program emphasizes foods high in vitamins, trace minerals, and substances thought to be active in diminishing disease risks. From that baseline, staff members tailor precise nutrition plans, uti-lizing the exchange list of the Block Nutrition Program, to reflect personal needs — biological, social, and psychological — and tastes.

INDEX

Index

A

Acid/alkaline balance, 23
Adaptation, 9—10
Adenosine triphosphate
(ATP), 208
Adriatic-Style Red Snapper,
173
Aduki (Adzuki, Azuki), 35
Adzuki Bean Soup, 71
Aging process, protein in, 17
Almonds
Almond Cream, 180
Almond-Oat Crisps,
Apple Crisp, 197
Arame with Miso-Almond
Sauce over Soba, 161
Chestnut Cream Pie, 190
Granola, 177
Lime-Almond Dressing,
119
Miso-Almond Butter
Sauce, 156
Rice with Almonds and
Capers, 83
Wheatberry and Rice Pilaf,
93
Alzheimer's Disease, 45
Amasake, 25
Amasake Cream, 180
Anasazi, 35
Animal foods, 15—17, 207
Antibiotic residues in milk
products, 20
Appetizers See also **Dips;**
Spreads
Guacamole, 55
Hummus, 55
Spring Rolls, 56
Tapenade, 58
Tempeh Dip, 54
Tempeh-Stuffed Mush-
rooms, 56
Tofu "Cheese," 54
Tofu Dip, 57
Apples
Apple-Corn Slices, 198

Apple Crêpes with Cara-
mel Sauce, 196
Apple Crisp, 197
Apple Glaze, 185
Apple Tart, 190
Baked Apples with Filling,
196
Cinnamon Apple Glaze,
191
Dried Fruit Compote, 177
Poached Apple Slices, 184
Arame See also **Sea Vegetables**
Arame and Cabbage
Sauté, 160
Arame, Broccoli, and Car-
rot Salad, 160
Arame with Mirin and
Lime, 161
Arame with Miso-Almond
Sauce over Soba, 161
Arctium lappa, 41
Asparagus with Chinese Black
Bean Sauce, 135

B

Baked Apples with Filling, 196
Baked Greens, 135
Baked Rice Pilaf, 88
Baked Squash Pureé, 141
Baked Tofu Cutlets, 122
Barley, 25—26
Mushroom-Barley Soup, 65
Wheatberry and Barley
Salad, 92
Basic Brown Rice, 82
Basic Brown Sauce, 158
Basic Bulgur, 94
Basic Dried Pasta, 106
Basic Fish Stock, 77
Basic Quinoa, 102
Basic Seitan, 129
Basic Teff, 105
Basic Vegetable Stock, 60
Basic White Cake, 199
Basmati Rice with Black-Eyed
Peas, 86
Beans, 33—38
Adzuki Bean Soup, 71

Black Bean and Corn Salad,
112
Black Bean Soup, 73
Black Beans with Hiziki,
115
Green Beans with Dill
Vinaigrette, 147
Kidney Beans with Lime-
Almond Dressing, 118
Minestrone, 71
Mixed Bean Salad, 114
Navy Bean and Sweet
Corn Soup, 74
Refried Beans, 112
White Bean Salad, 119
Beri-Beri, 25
Berries
Berry Sauce, 181
Strawberry Pudding, 182
Strawberry Mousse, 182
Strawberry Tart with Kuzu
Glaze, 186
Black Beans, 35
Black Bean and Corn Salad,
112
Black Bean Soup, 73
Black Beans with Hiziki, 115
Black-eyed peas , 35
Basmati Rice with Black-
Eyed Peas, 86
Black-Eyed Peas and Rice,
113
Black Soybeans, 35
Blanched Vegetable Salad, 138
Block nutrition program, 206
origins and rationale, 206
principal of homeostasis in,
207—9
Breads See also **Muffins**
Chapatis (Pan-Grilled
Flatbreads), 97
Cornbread, 99
Crêpes, 197
Injera, 106
Tofu Cornbread, 100
Broccoli
Arame, Broccoli, and Car-
rot Salad, 160

Gingered Pasta Salad, 109
Seitan Kebabs, 129
Seitan-Vegetable Medley,
    131
Tofu Fettucini, 122
Vegetable-Fried Rice, 90
Brownies, 194
Brown Rice Salad, 84
Brown Rice Timbales, 86
Buckwheat, 30–31
Buckwheat Pilaf, 102
Buckwheat Salad, 101
Buckwheat Tabouli, 101
Bulgur, 27
Basic Bulgur, 94
Bulgur Muffins, 178
Homestyle Bulgur, 94
Tabouli, 94
Tofu-Bulgur Burger, 124
Vegetable-Fried Rice, 90
Burdock root, 41
Butter Beans, 36
Buying sources, 50

C
Cabbage
Arame and Cabbage
    Sauté, 160
Cabbage-Fennel Soup, 64
Cabbage-Tempeh Sauté,
    137
Lemony Watercress Pin-
    wheels, 136
Lentil-Stuffed Cabbage
    Rolls, 117
Pressed Cabbage Salad,
    145
Stuffed Age Pouches, 125
Cakes *See also* **Cookies; Des-
serts; Fillings; Pastries; Pies;
Puddings; Toppings**
Basic White Cake, 199
Carob Cake, 200
Carrot Cake, 198
Calcium, 17–18
Cancer, diet in, 6, 15–17, 19
Canola oil, 19
Carbohydrates, 21–22

Carob
Carob Cake, 200
Carob-Frosted Brownies,
    194
Carob Frosting, 194
Crab Chip Cookies, 192
Carrots
Arame, Broccoli, and Car-
    rot Salad, 160
Blanched Vegetable Salad,
    138
Carrot Bisque with Curry, 77
Carrot Cake, 198
Carrot-Daikon Salad, 146
Polenta with Carrot Sauce,
    99
Seitan Kebabs, 129
Seitan Pot Pie, 131
Seitan-Vegetable Medley,
    131
Sesame-Veggie Salad, 146
Udon Noodles with Carrot-
    Basil Sauce, 107
Vegetables á la Grecque,
    142
Cauliflower
Blanched Vegetable Salad,
    138
Cauliflower Sauté, 137
Seitan-Vegetable Medley,
    131
Sesame-Veggie Salad, 146
Vegetables á la Grecque,
    142
Cecis *See* **Chickpeas**
Chapatis (Pan-Grilled
    Flatbreads), 97
Chestnuts
Chestnut Cream Pie, 190
Chestnut Purée, 189
Chickpeas, 36
Chickpea-Millet Patties, 90
Chickpea Potage, 71
Chickpea Salad, 113
Chickpea Soup, 72
Hummus, 55
Leek Soup in Chickpea
    Broth, 64

Saffron Brown Rice, 84
Vegetables á la Grecque,
    142
China Project, 16, 18, 19
Cholesterol, 25
Chromium, 21–22
Cinnamon Apple Glaze, 191
Cookies *See also* **Cakes; Des-
serts; Fillings; Pastries; Pies;
Puddings; Toppings**
Almond-Oat Crisps, 193
Carob-Frosted Brownies,
    194
Crab Chip Cookies, 192
Oatmeal-Sesame-Raisin
    Cookies, 191
Peanut Butter Cookies, 193
Cooking equipment, 45
Corn, 29–30
Apple-Corn Slices, 198
Arame with Mirin and
    Lime, 161
Black Bean and Corn Salad,
    112
Cornbread, 99
Corn Chowder, 68
Cornmeal Pudding, 195
Navy Bean and Sweet
    Corn Soup, 75
Polenta, Plain and Simple,
    98
Polenta with Carrot Sauce,
    99
Polenta with Mushrooms,
    98
Tofu Cornbread, 100
Cornbread, 99
Cornmeal Pudding, 195
Couscous, 27
Couscous-Red Pepper
    Salad, 96
Couscous Salad, 95
Couscous with Vegetables
    and Seitan, 96
Sweet Couscous Tart with
    Fruit Filling, 184
Cracked wheat, 27
Creamy Cucumber Soup, 75

Creamy Mushroom Soup, 68
Cucumbers
  Buckwheat Salad, 101
  Chickpea Salad, 113
  Couscous-Red Pepper
    Salad, 96
  Creamy Cucumber Soup, 76
  Cucumber Cilantro Salad,
    145
  Garden Quinoa Salad, 102
  Sesame-Veggie Salad, 146

D
Daikon, 41
  Carrot-Daikon Salad, 146
Dairy products, 19–21
Desserts See also **Cakes;
Cookies; Fillings; Pastries;
Pies; Puddings; Toppings**
  Apple-Corn Slices, 198
  Apple Crêpes with Cara-
    mel Sauce, 196
  Baked Apples with Filling,
    196
  Dried Fruit Compote, 177
  Fruit Filling with Glaze, 186
  Fruit Kanten (Fruit Gel), 178
  Granola, 177
  Poached Apple Slices, 184
  Popcorn & Peanut Crunch,
    195
  Profiterôles, 179
Diabetes, 21–22
Diet, in disease prevention and
  treatment, 6, 15–17
Diet-linked disease, excess as
  cause of, 14–15
Dips See also **Appetizers;
Spreads**
  Guacamole, 55
  Hummus, 55
  Tempeh Dip, 54
  Tofu Dip, 57
Disease, prevention and treat
  ment in diet, 6, 15–17
Dressings
  Lemon Olive-Oil Dressing,
    96

Lime Dressing, 119
Lime-Miso-Mustard Dress-
  ing, 152
Lime Salad Dressing, 150
Miso Dressings, 152
Mustard Vinaigrette Dress-
  ing, 83
Olive Oil Vinaigrette, 85,
  114
Orange-Dijon Dressing, 88
Orange-Ginger Vinaigrette,
  155
Red Lentil Vinaigrette, 116
Sesame Dressing, 147, 164
Sesame-Umeboshi Dress-
  ing, 153
Simple Vinaigrette, 154
Sweet Miso Salad Dress-
  ing, 151
Tahini Dressing, 157
Three Flavors Dressing,
  150
Tofu Mayonnaise, 151
Tofu Salad Dressing, 154
Dried Fruit Compote, 177

E
Efficiency strategies, 44–45
Ergosterol, 40
Exotica, 41

F
Fats, 18–19
Fillings See also **Desserts; Past-
ries; Pies; Puddings; Toppings**
  Almond Cream, 180
  Amasake Cream, 180
  Chestnut Purée, 189
  Vanilla Malted Cream, 179
Fish
  Adriatic-Style Red Snapper,
    173
  Basic Fish Stock, 77
  Fish Dumplings, 78
  Fish Dumpling Soup, 78
  Grilled Striped Bass with
    Lime-Mustard Mari-
    nade, 172

Grilled Tuna Salad, 168
Kombu and Bonito Flake
  Soup, 78
Orange-Marinated Fish,
  171
Oven-Poached Sea Bass,
  169
Provincial Fish Soup, 79
Rainbow Trout Dijon, 173
Sautéed Trout, 171
Stuffed Rainbow Trout with
  Tofu Sauce, 170
Sweet and Sour Salmon
  with Peapods, 168
Thai-Style White Fish, 174
Whole Steamed Fish, 169
Folic acid, 23
Food selection, guidelines for,
  8–11
Fordhooks, 36
French Onion Soup with
  Herbed Croutons, 61
Fruit
  Fruit Filling with Glaze, 186
  Fruit Kanten (Fruit Gel),
    178
  Sweet Couscous Tart with
    Fruit Filling, 184
Fu "Stew," 133

G
Gallstones, 22
Garbangos. See Chickpeas
Garden Quinoa Salad, 102
Garnishes
  Herbed Croutons, 61
  Kombu Condiment, 162
Gingered Pasta Salad, 109
Ginger-Kuzu Sauce, 126
Gingery Millet Soup, 66
Granola, 177
Great Northern Beans, 36
Green beans
  Green Beans with Dill
    Vinaigrette, 147
  Vegetables á la Grecque,
    142
Green Onion-Kuzu Sauce, 154

Greens Rolled in Nori, 166
Grilled Striped Bass with Lime-Mustard Marinade, 172
Grilled Tuna Salad, 168
Guacamole, 55

H
Herbed Croutons, 61
High density lipoproteins (HDLs), 23
Hiziki, 40. *See also* **Sea Vegetables**
   Black Beans with Hiziki, 115
   Hiziki-Mushroom Sauté, 164
   Hiziki Salad, 163
   Hiziki with Onions and Mushrooms, 164
Homeostasis, 207–9
Homestyle Bulgur, 94
Homogenization, 21
Horseradish Sauce, 156
Hot and Sour Soup, 63
Hot Tempeh Slices, 126
Hummus, 55
Hyperactivity, 21

I
Immune system, role of whole grains in, 23–24
Injera, 106
Iodine, 27
Italian Quinoa Salad, 103

K
Kale
   Baked Greens, 135
   Kale-Stuffed Onions, 139
Kidney beans, 36
   Kidney Beans with Lime-Almond Dressing, 118–19
   Minestrone, 71
   Refried Beans, 112
Kombu, 40 *See also* **Sea Vegetables**
   Kombu and Bonito Flake Soup, 78

Kombu Condiment, 162
Kombu Logs, 162
Kuzu Sauce, 123

L
Lactase, 20
Leeks
   Blanched Vegetable Salad, 138
   Leek Soup in Chickpea Broth, 64
Legumes, 27, 33–38. *See also* **Beans**
Lemon
   Lemon Custard, 188
   Lemon Olive-Oil Dressing, 96
   Lemony Watercress Pinwheels, 136
Lentils, 36
   Cilantro-Lentil Salad, 118
   Lentil-Noodle Soup, 69
   Lentil Pâté, 115
   Lentil Soup, 68
   Lentil-Stuffed Cabbage Rolls, 117
   Nutty Lentil Salad, 118
   Red Lentil Salad, 116
   Red Lentil Vinaigrette, 116
Leukotrienes, 18
Lima Beans, 36
Lime
   Lime-Almond Dressing, 119
   Lime-Miso-Mustard Dressing, 152
   Lime Salad Dressing, 150
Low density lipoproteins (LDLs), 23
Lysine, 27

M
Macrobiotic approach, 206–7
Meal, composing, 42–44
Meal Plans, 202–5
Milk, 19–21
Millet, 26
   Chickpea-Millet Patties, 90

Gingery Millet Soup, 66
Millet Stew, 91
Millet with Sautéed Vegetables, 91
Saffron Millet Pilaf, 92
Vegetable-Fried Rice, 90
Minestrone, 70
Miso, 38–39
   Arame with Miso-Almond Sauce over Soba, 161
   Lime-Miso-Mustard Dressing, 152
   Miso-Almond Butter Sauce, 156
   Miso Dressings, 152
   Miso Soup, 62
   Peanut Miso Sauce, 157
   Sweet Miso Salad Dressing, 151
Mixed Bean Salad, 114
Mochi, 25
Muffins *See also* **Breads**
   Bulgur Muffins, 178
   Sweet Potato Muffins, 183
Mushrooms *See also* **Shiitake Mushrooms**
   Adzuki Bean Soup, 72
   Brown Rice Timbales, 86
   Creamy Mushroom Soup, 67
   Fu "Stew," 133
   Hiziki-Mushroom Sauté, 164
   Hiziki with Onions and Mushrooms, 164
   Mushroom-Barley Soup, 65
   Mushroom-Kuzu Sauce, 157
   Mushroom Topping, 99
   Polenta with Mushrooms, 98
   Seitan Kebabs, 129
   Seitan Stroganoff, 130
   Stuffed Rainbow Trout with Tofu Sauce, 170
   Tempeh-Stuffed Mushrooms, 56
   Tempeh-Stuffed Onions, 140

Mushrooms (continued)
Tofu Fettucini, 122
Vegetable-Fried Rice, 90
Vegetable Rice Pilaf and
Stuffing, 82
Vegetables á la Grecque,
142
Wild Rice and Mushroom
Soup, 65
Mustard Vinaigrette Dressing,
83

N
Navy Beans, 37
Navy Bean and Sweet
Corn Soup, 74
Niacin, 25
Nightshade vegetable group,
caution regarding, 22—23
Noodle Pancakes, 108
Nutritional adequacy, question
of, 10—11
Nutty Lentil Salad, 118

O
Oatmeal-Sesame-Raisin Cook-
ies, 191
Oats, 28
Almond-Oat Crisps, 193
Apple Crisp, 197
Crab Chip Cookies, 192
Oatmeal-Sesame-Raisin
Cookies, 191
Oils, 18—19
Olive Oil Vinaigrette, 85, 114
Omega-3 fatty acids, 18—19
Omega-6 fatty acids, 18
Onions
French Onion Soup with
Herbed Croutons, 61
Kale-Stuffed Onions, 139
Savory Onion Tart, 138
Tempeh-Stuffed Onions,
140
Oranges
Orange-Dijon Dressing, 88
Orange-Ginger Vinaigrette,
155

Orange-Marinated Fish,
171
Oven-Poached Sea Bass, 169

P
Pantothenic acid, 23
Pasta
Arame with Miso-Almond
Sauce over Soba, 161
Baked Rice Pilaf, 88
Basic Dried Pasta, 106
Gingered Pasta Salad, 109
Lentil-Noodle Soup, 69
Minestrone, 70
Noodle Pancakes, 108
Pasta with Peanut Sauce,
109
Pasta with Tofu and Pea
Pods, 110
Soba with Kombu Broth,
107
Soba with Shiitake Broth,
106
Stuffed Age Pouches, 125
Tofu Fettucini, 122
Udon Noodles with Carrot-
Basil Sauce, 107
Pastries. See also **Cakes; Cook-
ies; Desserts; Fillings; Pies**
Lentil Pâté, 115
Pressed Oat Crust, 186
Profiterôles, 179
Whole Wheat Pie Crust,
185
Peanut Butter
Pasta with Peanut Sauce,
109
Peanut Butter Cookies, 193
Peanut Miso Sauce, 157
Peanuts: Popcorn & Peanut
Crunch, 195
Peapods
Pasta with Tofu and
Peapods, 110
Sweet and Sour Salmon
with Peapods, 168
Pecans
Crab Chip Cookies, 192

Pumpkin Tart with Glazed
Pecans, 188
Wild Rice Pilaf, 87
Peptic ulcers, 22
Phosphorus, 18
Pies See also **Cakes; Desserts;
Fillings; Pastries**
savory
Hiziki Tart, 165
Onion Tart, 138
Seitan Pot Pie, 131
sweet
Apple Crisp, 197
Apple Tart, 190
Chestnut Cream Pie,
190
Pumpkin Pie, 187
Pumpkin Tart with
Glazed Pecans, 188
Squash Pie, 189
Strawberry Tart with
Kuzu Glaze, 186
Sweet Couscous Tart
with Fruit Filling, 184
Pinto beans, 37
Minestrone, 71
Refried Beans, 112
Poached Apple Slices, 184
Polenta
Polenta, Plain and Simple,
98
Polenta with Carrot Sauce,
99
Polenta with Mushrooms,
98
Popcorn & Peanut Crunch, 195
Pressed Cabbage Salad, 145
Pressed Oat Crust, 186
Profiteroles, 179
Prostaglandin E2, 18
Protein, excess, as risk factor,
16—17
Provincial Fish Soup, 79
Puddings. See also **Desserts;
Fillings; Pastries; Toppings**
Cornmeal Pudding, 195
Lemon Custard, 188
Rice Pudding, 181

Strawberry Pudding, 182
Strawberry Mousse, 182
Sweet Potato Pudding, 183
Pumpkin
Pumpkin Pie, 187
Pumpkin Seed Sauce, 151
Pumpkin Tart with Glazed
Pecans, 188
Pyridoxine, 23

Q
Quinoa, 31–32
Basic Quinoa, 102
Garden Quinoa Salad, 102
Italian Quinoa Salad, 103
Quinoa with Seitan, 104
Saffron Quinoa, 104–5

R
Rainbow Trout
Rainbow Trout Dijon, 173
Sautéed Trout, 171
Stuffed Rainbow Trout with
Tofu Sauce, 170
Raisins
Carrot Cake, 198
Dried Fruit Compote, 177
Oatmeal-Sesame-Raisin
Cookies, 191
Recommended foods, 23
barley, 25–26
beans (legumes), 33
buckwheat, 30–31
corn, 29–30
millet, 26
miso, 38–39
oats, 28
quinoa, 31–32
rice, 24–25
rye, 28–29
teff, 32–33
wheat, 26–27
whole grains, 23–24
Red Lentils, 36
Red Lentil Salad, 116
Red Lentil Vinaigrette, 116
Seitan Fajitas, 132
Refried Beans, 112

Rice, 24–25
Baked Rice Pilaf, 88
baking, 82
Basic Brown Rice, 82
Basmati Rice with Black-
Eyed Peas, 86
Black-Eyed Peas and Rice,
113
boiling, 82
Brown Rice Salad, 84
Brown Rice Timbales, 86
Lentil-Stuffed Cabbage
Rolls, 117
pressure-cooked, 45, 82
Rice Patties, 89
Rice Pudding, 181
Rice with Almonds and
Capers, 83
Saffron Brown Rice, 84
Saffron Brown Rice Salad,
85
Stuffed Rainbow Trout with
Tofu Sauce, 170
Sweet Brown Rice Dump-
lings, 88
Vegetable-Fried Rice, 90
Vegetable Rice Pilaf and
Stuffing, 82
Wheatberry and Rice Pilaf,
93
Wild Rice and Mushroom
Soup, 65
Wild Rice Pilaf, 87
Rye, 28–29

S
Saffron
Saffron Brown Rice, 84
Saffron Brown Rice Salad,
85
Saffron Millet Pilaf, 92
Saffron Quinoa, 104
Salad dressings *See* **Dressings**
Salads
Arame, Broccoli, and Car-
rot Salad, 160
Black Bean and Corn Salad,
112

Blanched Vegetable Salad,
138
Brown Rice Salad, 84
Buckwheat Salad, 101
Buckwheat Tabouli, 101
Carrot-Daikon Salad, 146
Chickpea Salad, 113
Couscous-Red Pepper
Salad, 96
Couscous Salad, 95
Cucumber Cilantro Salad,
145
Fresh Cilantro, 118
Garden Quinoa Salad,
102
Gingered Pasta Salad, 109
Green Beans with Dill
Vinaigrette, 147
Grilled Tuna Salad, 168
Hiziki Salad, 163
Italian Quinoa Salad, 103
Mixed Bean Salad, 114
Nutty Lentil Salad, 118
Pressed Cabbage Salad,
145
Red Lentil Salad, 116
Saffron Brown Rice Salad,
85
Sesame-Veggie Salad, 146
Tabouli, 94
Tempeh Salad, 127
Turnips in Raspberry-Lime
Vinaigrette, 147
Wheatberry and Barley
Salad, 92
White Bean Salad, 119
Sauces
Basic Brown Sauce, 158
Berry Sauce, 181
Carmel Sauce, 197
Carrot Sauce, 99
Ginger-Kuzu Sauce, 126
Green Onion-Kuzu Sauce,
154
Horseradish-Dill Sauce,
156
Horseradish Sauce, 156
Kuzu Sauce, 123

Sauces (*continued*)
Miso-Almond Butter
   Sauce, 156
Mushroom-Kuzu Sauce,
   157
Mushroom Topping, 99
Peanut Miso Sauce, 157
Ponzu Sauce, 150
Pumpkin Seed Sauce, 151
Savory Olive Oil Sauce,
   152
Sesame-Citrus Marinade,
   153
Shoyu-Ginger Dipping
   Sauce, 150
Tofu-Dill Sauce, 175
Tofu Sauce, 171
Sautéed Trout, 171
Savory Olive Oil Sauce, 152
Scotch oats, 28
Scrambled Tofu, 124
Sea Vegetables, 40
Arame, Broccoli, and Car-
   rot Salad, 160
Arame and Cabbage
   Sauté, 160
Arame with Mirin and
   Lime, 161
Arame with Miso-Almond
   Sauce over Soba, 161
Black Beans with Hiziki,
   115
Cabbage-Fennel Soup, 64
Fish Dumpling Soup, 79
Greens Rolled in Nori, 166
Hiziki-Mushroom Sauté,
   164
Hiziki Salad, 163
Hiziki with Onions and
   Mushrooms, 164
Kombu and Bonito Flake
   Soup, 78
Kombu Condiment, 162
Kombu Logs, 162
Miso Soup, 63
Savory Hiziki Tart, 165
Soba with Kombu Broth,
   107

Vegetables á la Grecque,
   142
Wakame-Sesame Season-
   ing, 156
Seitan
Basic Seitan, 129
Couscous with Vegetables
   and Seitan, 96
Quinoa with Seitan, 104
Seitan Fajitas, 132
Seitan Kebabs, 129
Seitan Pot Pie, 131
Seitan Stroganoff, 130
Seitan-Vegetable Medley,
   131
Semolina, 27
Sesame
Oatmeal-Sesame-Raisin
   Cookies, 191
Pressed Oat Crust, 186
Sesame-Citrus Marinade,
   153
Sesame Dressing, 147, 164
Sesame Salt, 155
Sesame-Umeboshi Dress-
   ing, 153
Sesame-Veggie Salad, 146
Tahini Dressing, 157
Wakame-Sesame Season-
   ing, 156
Shiitake Mushrooms, 41 *See
also* **Mushrooms**
Hot and Sour Soup, 64
Millet Stew, 91
Miso Soup, 63
Mushroom-Barley Soup, 66
Noodle Pancakes, 108
Soba with Shiitake Broth,
   106
Spring Rolls, 56
Stuffed Age Pouches, 125
Tofu Egg-Foo Young, 123
Shoyu-Ginger Dipping Sauce,
   150
Shredded Brussels Sprouts, 136
Simple Vinaigrette, 154
Sodium containing foods, 16,
   39

Soups
Adzuki Bean Soup, 71
Basic Fish Stock, 77
Basic Vegetable Stock, 60
Black Bean Soup, 73
Cabbage-Fennel Soup, 63
Carrot Bisque with Curry,
   76
Chickpea Potage, 71
Chickpea Soup, 72
Corn Chowder, 68
Creamy Cucumber Soup,
   75
Creamy Mushroom Soup,
   67
Fish Dumpling Soup, 78
French Onion Soup with
   Herbed Croutons, 61
Gingery Millet Soup, 66
Hot and Sour Soup, 63
Kombu and Bonito Flake
   Soup, 77
Leek Soup in Chickpea
   Broth, 64
Lentil-Noodle Soup, 69
Lentil Soup, 68
Minestrone, 70
Miso Soup, 62
Mushroom-Barley Soup, 65
Navy Bean and Sweet
   Corn Soup, 74
Provincial Fish Soup, 79
Soba with Kombu Broth,
   107
Soba with Shiitake Broth,
   106
Split Pea Soup, 73
Squash Potage, 67
Vegetable Soup, 60
Wild Rice and Mushroom
   Soup, 65
Yellow Split Pea Potage, 75
Soybeans, 37–38
Spaghetti Squash with Sesame
   Sauce, 142
Split peas, 38
Split Pea Soup, 73
Yellow Split Pea Potage, 75

Spreads. *See also* **Appetizers; Dips**
Lentil Pâté, 115
Tempeh Pâté, 126
Tofu "Cheese," 54
Spring Rolls, 56
Squash
Baked Squash Pureé, 141
Fu "Stew," 133
Spaghetti Squash with Sesame Sauce, 142
Squash Pie, 189
Squash Soup, 67
Squash with Onions and Almonds, 140
Strawberries
Strawberry Pudding, 182
Strawberry Tart with Kuzu Glaze, 186
Strawberry Mousse, 182
Stuffed Age Pouches, 125
Stuffed Rainbow Trout with Tofu Sauce, 170
Sugar, 21–22
Sulfamethazine, 20
Sunflower Seeds
Baked Rice Pilaf, 88
Buckwheat Pilaf, 102
Cornmeal Pudding, 195
Sweet and Sour Salmon with Peapods, 168
Sweet Brown Rice Dumplings, 88
Sweet Couscous Tart with Fruit Filling, 184
Sweet Miso Salad Dressing, 151
Sweet Potatoes
Sweet Potato Muffins, 183
Sweet Potato Pudding, 183
Sweet vegetables, 22

T
Tabouli, 94
Tahini Dressing, 157
Tapenade, 58
Teff, 32–33
Basic Teff, 105

Injera, 106
Teff Patties, 105
Tempeh, 37
Cabbage-Tempeh Sauté, 137
Hot Tempeh Slices, 126
Tempeh Dip, 54
Tempeh Pâté, 126
Tempeh Salad, 127
Tempeh-Stuffed Mushrooms, 56
Tempeh-Stuffed Onions, 140
Thai-Style White Fish, 174
Thiamine, 25
Three Flavors Dressing, 150
Tofu, 37–38
Baked Tofu Cutlets, 122
Hiziki-Mushroom Sauté, 164
Hiziki Salad, 163
Horseradish-Dill Sauce, 156
Horseradish Sauce, 156
Hot and Sour Soup, 63
Kale-Stuffed Onions, 139
Pasta with Tofu and Pea Pods, 110
Rainbow Trout Dijon, 173
Savory Hiziki Tart, 165
Scrambled Tofu, 124
Seitan Stroganoff, 130
Stuffed Age Pouches, 125
Tofu-Bulgur Burger, 124
Tofu "Cheese," 54
Tofu Cornbread, 100
Tofu-Dill Sauce, 175
Tofu Dip, 57
Tofu Egg-Foo Young, 123
Tofu Fettucini, 122
Tofu Mayonnaise, 151
Tofu Salad Dressing, 154
Tofu Sauce, 171
Tomatoes, 22–23
Tooth decay, 21
Toppings. *See also* **Desserts; Fillings; Pastries; Pies; Puddings**
Apple Glaze, 185

Carob Frosting, 194
Cinnamon Apple Glaze, 191
Tryptophan, 27
Turnips in Raspberry-Lime Vinaigrette, 147
Turtle beans, 35

U
Udon Noodles with Carrot-Basil Sauce, 107
Ulcer, 22–23

V
Vanilla Malted Cream, 179
Vegetables *See also* **Sea Vegetables; Specific vegetables**
Asparagus with Chinese Black Bean Sauce, 135
Baked Greens, 135
Baked Squash Pureé, 141
Basic Vegetable Stock, 60
Black Bean Soup, 73
Blanched Vegetable Salad, 138
Brown Rice Salad, 84
Cabbage-Fennel Soup, 64
Cabbage-Tempeh Sauté, 137
Cauliflower Sauté, 137
Couscous Salad, 95
Couscous with Vegetables and Seitan, 96
Gingery Millet Soup, 67
Greens Rolled in Nori, 166
Italian Quinoa Salad, 103
Kale-Stuffed Onions, 139
Leek Soup in Chickpea Broth, 64
Lemony Watercress Pinwheels, 136
Millet Stew, 91
Millet with Sautéed Vegetables, 91
Minestrone, 70
nightshade group of, 22–23
Provincial Fish Soup, 79

Vegetables (continued)
  Savory Onion Tart, 138
  Seitan Pot Pie, 131
  Seitan-Vegetable Medley,
    131
  Sesame-Veggie Salad, 146
  Shredded Brussels Sprouts,
    136
  Spaghetti Squash with
    Sesame Sauce, 142
  Squash with Onions and
    Almonds, 140
  Tabouli, 94
  Tempeh-Stuffed Onions,
    140
  Vegetable-Fried Rice, 90
  Vegetable Rice Pilaf and
    Stuffing, 82
  Vegetables á la Grecque,
    142
  Vegetable Soup, 60

W
Wakame-Sesame Seasoning,
  156
Watercress
  Baked Greens, 135
  Lemony Watercress Pin
    wheels, 136
Wheat, 26—27
Wheatberries
  Wheatberry and Barley
    Salad, 92
  Wheatberry and Rice Pilaf,
    93
White Bean Salad, 119
White fish
  Basic Fish Stock, 77
  Orange-Marinated Fish,
    171
  Oven-Poached Sea Bass,
    169
  Provincial Fish Soup, 79
  Thai-Style White Fish, 174
  Whole Steamed Fish, 169
Whole grains, 23—24
Whole Steamed Fish, 169
Whole Wheat Pie Crust, 185

Wild Rice and Mushroom
  Soup, 65
Wild Rice Pilaf, 87

X
Xanthine oxidase, 21

Y
Yellow Split Pea Potage, 75

Z
Zybilocin (dipicolinic acid), 39

Recipe Notes

Recipe Notes

Recipe Notes

Recipe Notes